Drone Art:
Low Altitude Landscapes

An  School Monograph

John Vigour

Drone Art:
Low Altitude Landscapes

John Vigour

University of Virginia School of Architecture, Charlottesville, 2014

Design: Cally Bryant
Editor: Cynthia Smith

Printed by the University of Virginia School of Architecture
© 2014, Rector and Visitors of the University of Virginia

University of Virginia School of Architecture
Campbell Hall PO Box 400122
Charlottesville, VA 22904

www.arch.virginia.edu

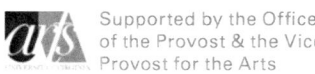

Supported by the Office of the Provost & the Vice Provost for the Arts

table of contents

foreword

Richard Guy Wilson
Commonwealth Professor and Chair,
Department of Architectural History,
University of Virginia, School of Architecture

The aerial photograph by John Vigour opens up a very exciting and new perspective on the static elements he captures below. His photographs are unique, compelling and beautiful and bring a new understanding of the landscape, buildings, statues and other objects that spread across the picture plain. The relationship of the parts to the whole, of the back to the front, of the side to the rear, of the garden to the house, or of a dog walker passing along are captured in his wide range of photographs.

There is a long history of the relationship of photography and architecture and/or buildings. Architecture has been one of the most persistent subjects of photography from its very beginnings back in the 1830s. Buildings are static and do not twitch or move as do human beings which created problems for the early cameras with their long exposure time. Photographs have been the means by which much of the world knows the pyramids, the Pantheon, or the Taj Mahal.

John Vigour shifts the traditionally static perspective of photography and buildings and allows us a new way of understanding. Utilizing what can be called a "drone" or a mobile model airplane called a "Quadcopter" with four propellers and electric motor which weighs two pounds, measures about 12 inches square and is remotely controlled, he attaches a camera and sets it off. Depending on the subject, the Quadcopter is slowly rotated while between 12 to 15 shots are taken and then cropped together. The maximum height is 200 feet and of course the higher one goes the more distortion occurs since you have a round earth and a flat piece of paper on which to print.

The photographs allow one to see connections and changes that are difficult to understand from a ground view. The difference in the layout of the gardens behind the pavilions at the University becomes apparent, as does how automobiles are hidden in the alleys leading to the Lawn. The differences between the highly geometrical layout of the plantings and public spaces in front of Alderman Library and Peabody Hall contrast with the more topographically controlled areas around the Architecture School and Drama building. In Williamsburg, the view of the Governor's Palace illuminates how the main building is served not just by the row of flankers in front, visible as you approach, but also the tremendous array of other structures off to the sides. This is where the slaves lived who allowed the Palace to function.

Not all of the photos are grand buildings, but also perspectives on roads, intersections and country corners which become memorable in Vigour's photographs. He has created a stunning panorama of the different landscapes we all occupy and how we might better understand them. And at the same time, the photographs are real works of art.

Why do birds flying attract the eye? Are we reminded of that third dimension, altitude? And how does the country-side appear from a bird's-eye view? These photographs of wide-angle panoramas, captured by a bird-sized model helicopter, display a delightful perspective of Virginia's beauty as never seen before. Viewed from an altitude just above the treetops, our neighborhoods and towns reveal mosaics in the context of their mountains and waterways. Besides hallmarking the novel technique, the composi-tions emphasize a classic balance of form and color.

Section One, The Grounds, displays the University of Virginia in intimate detail while uncovering hidden spatial relationships. The panoramas dazzle, with 360 degree landscapes of the Lawn and Grounds encompassing a perspective from the surrounding Ragged Mountains all the way down to passing pedestrians.

Section Two, The Virginia Countryside, wanders from mountain cliffs to estuaries as seen from altitudes of 25 to 250 feet. This small quiet helicopter has gracefully loitered over Williamsburg, Richmond, reservoirs, cemeteries, and highways. There are also several landscapes from atop tall poles poking up through trees that reveal views tantalizingly obscured to passersby.

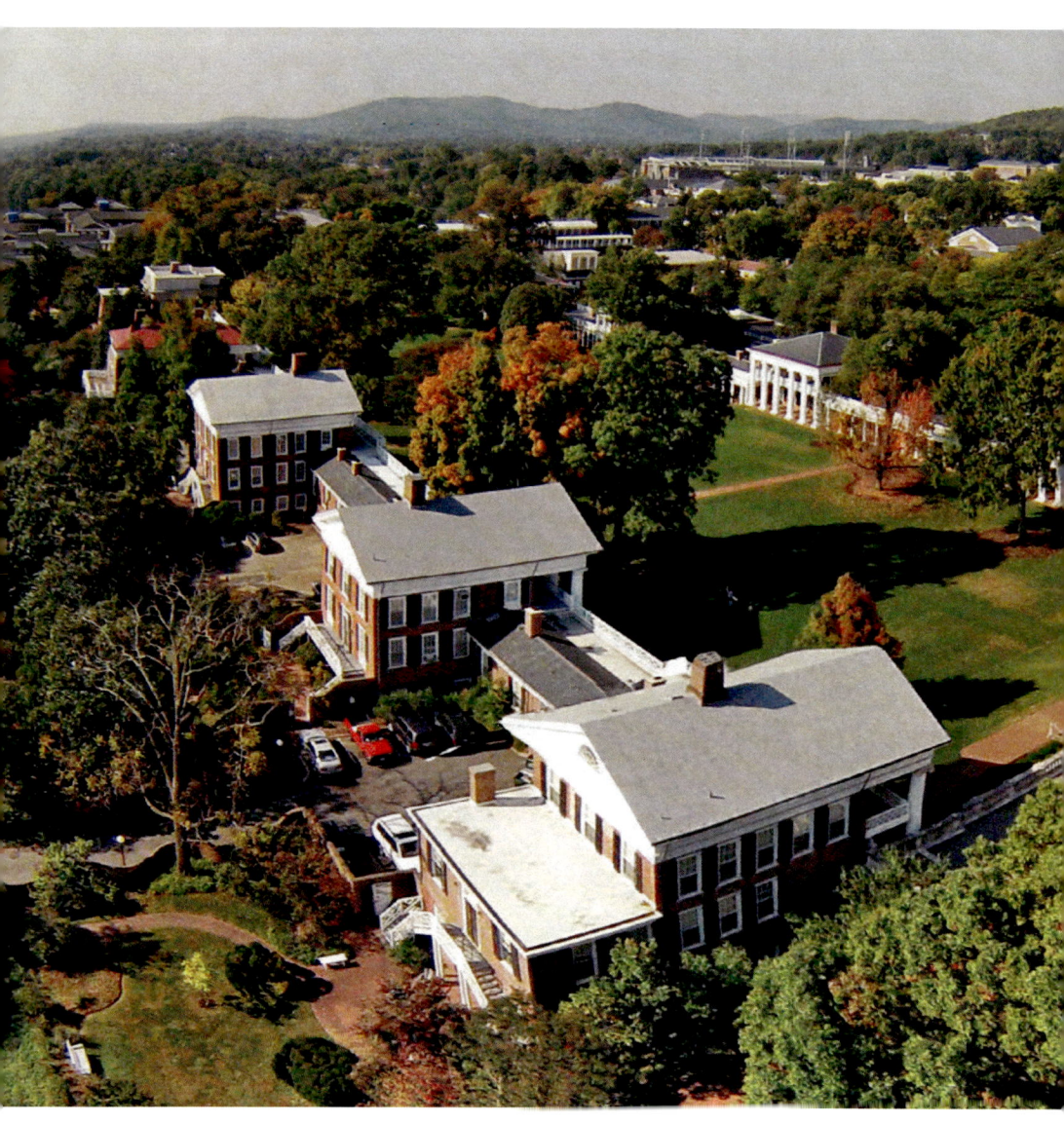

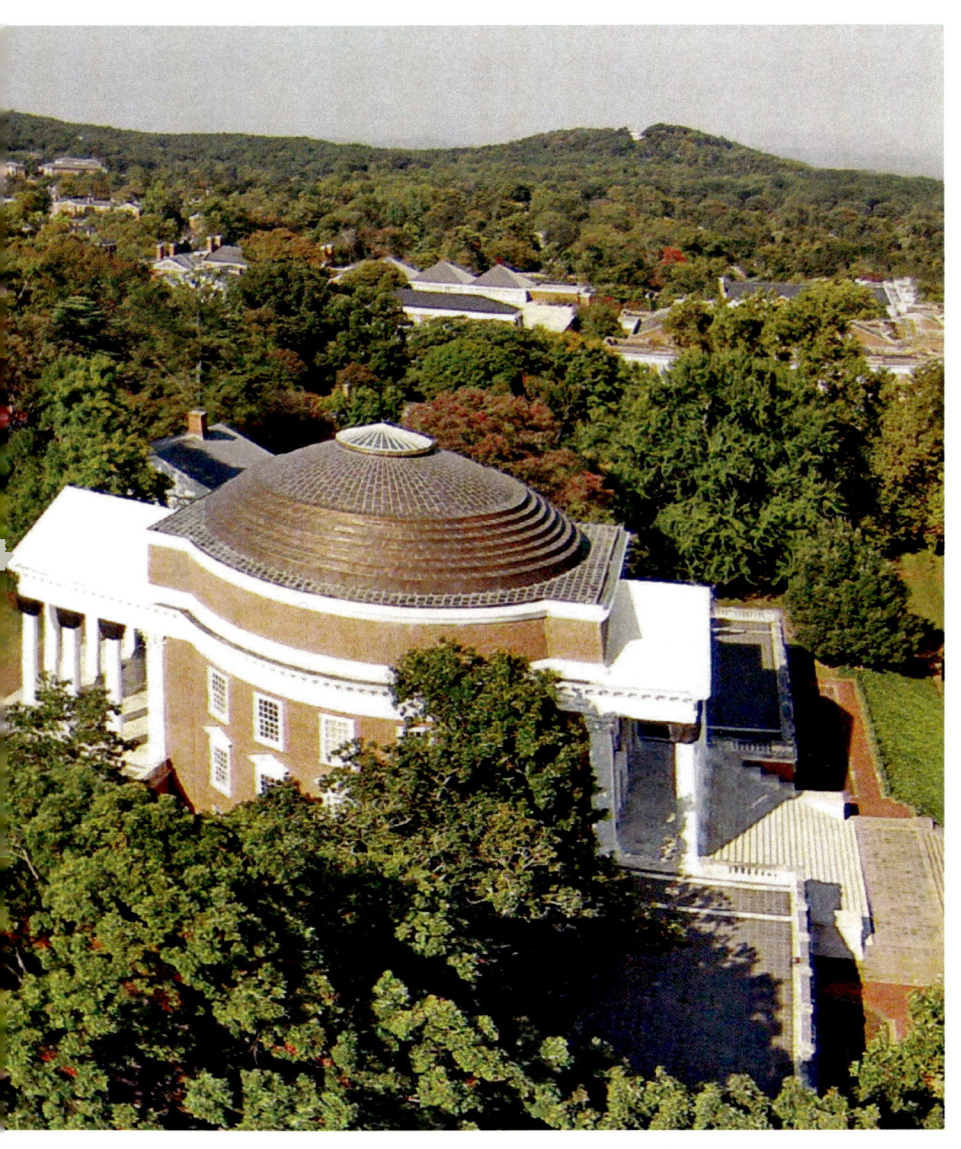

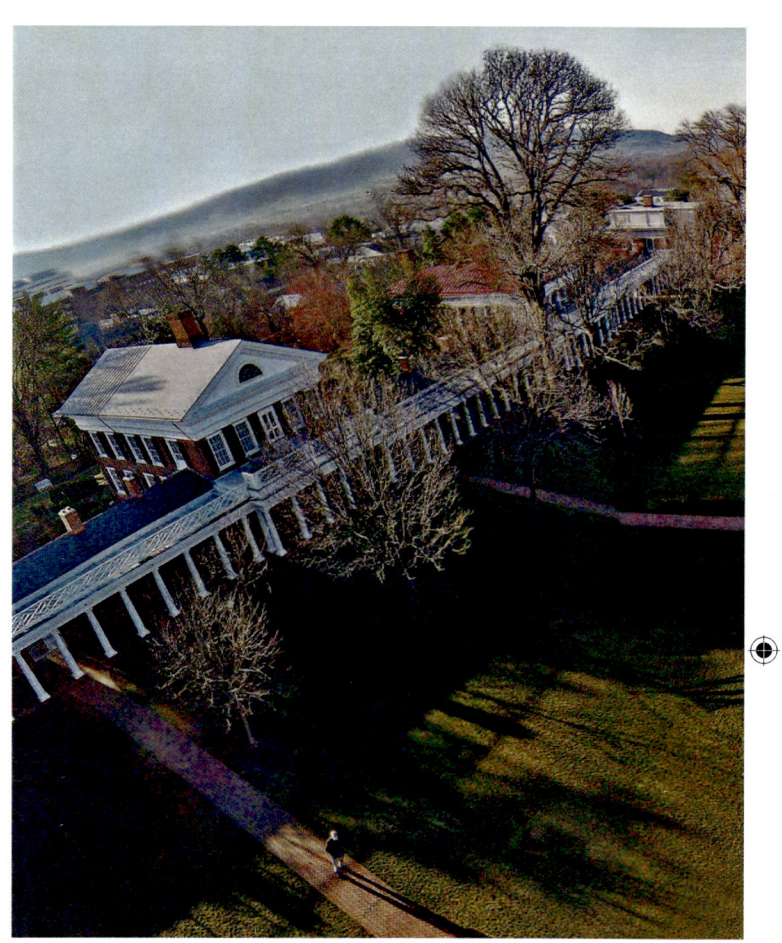

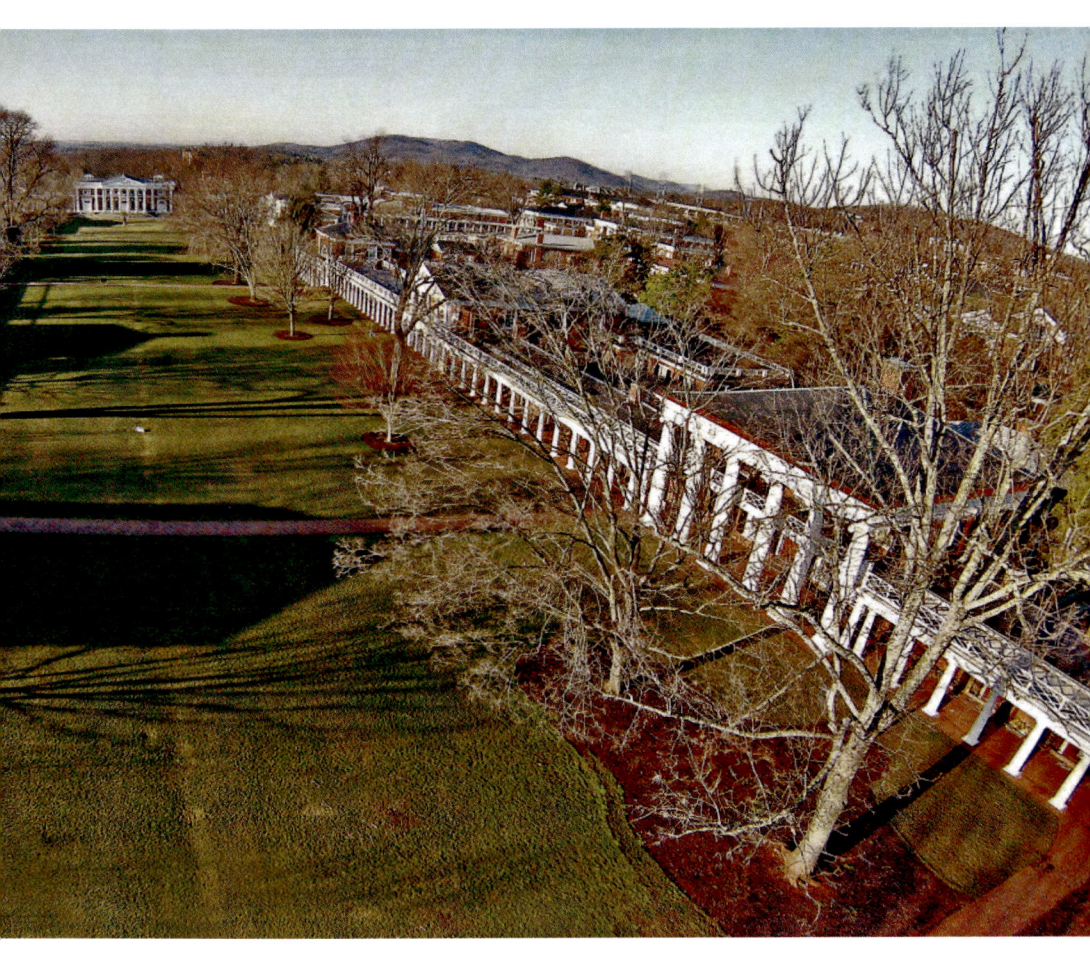

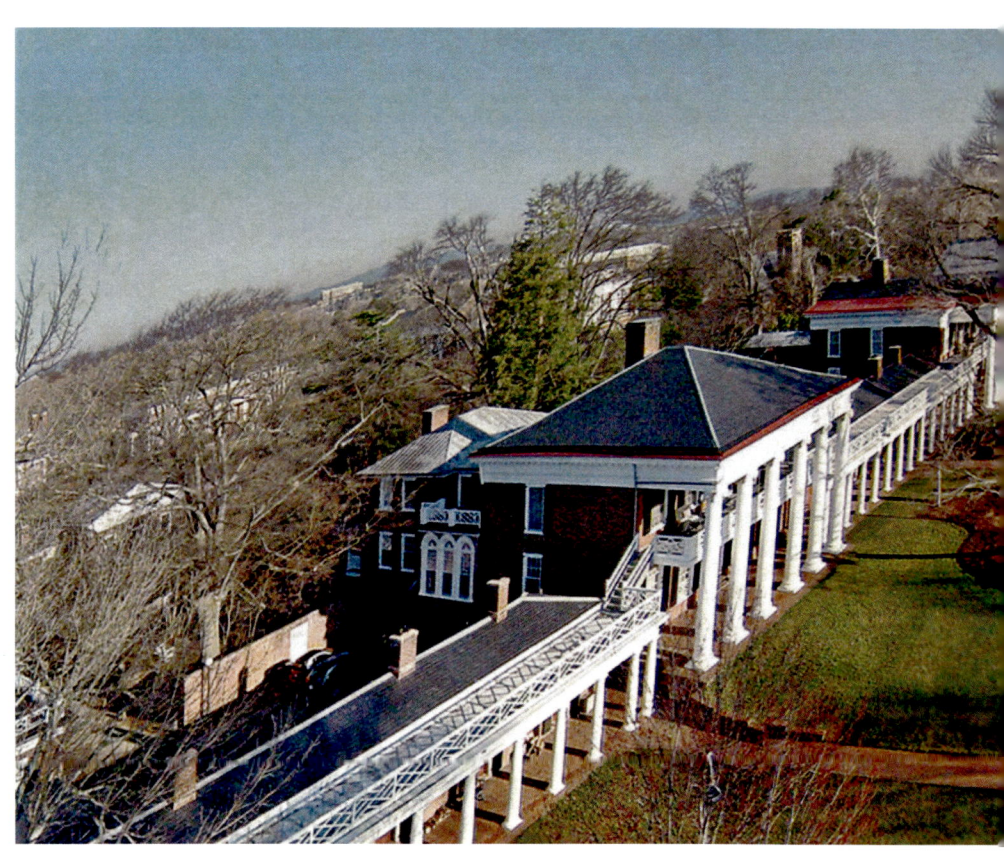

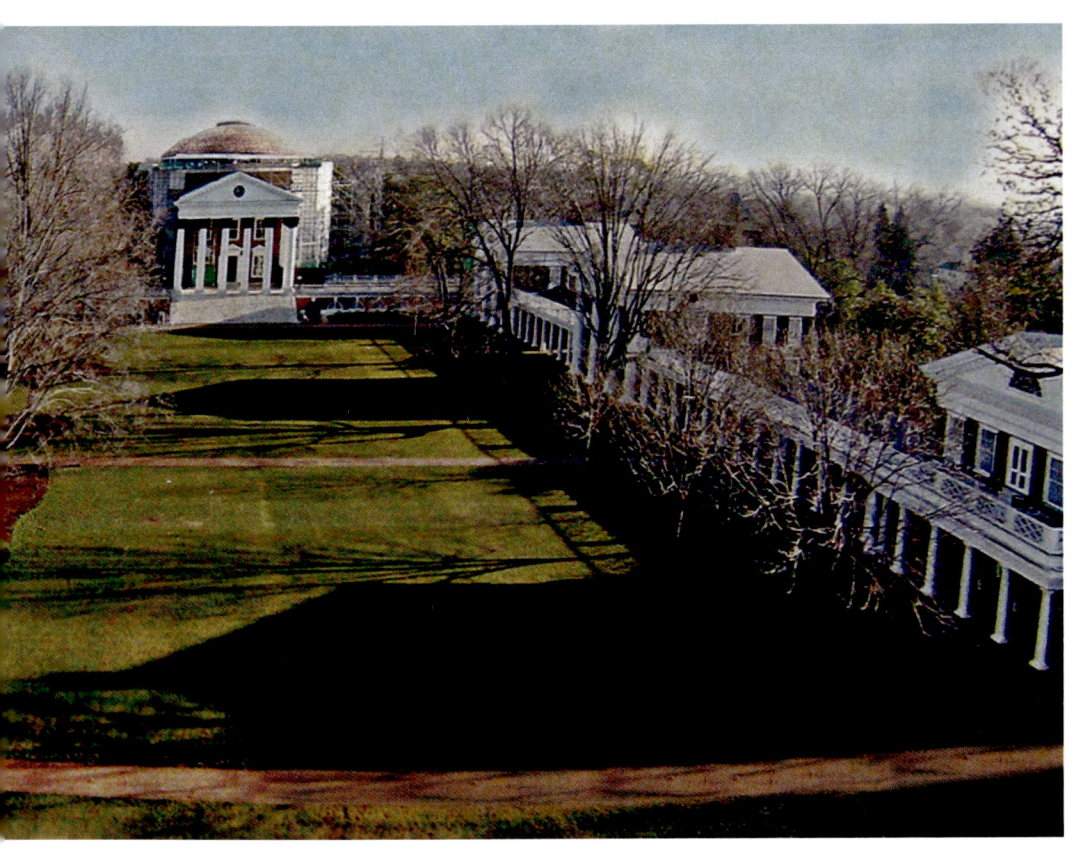

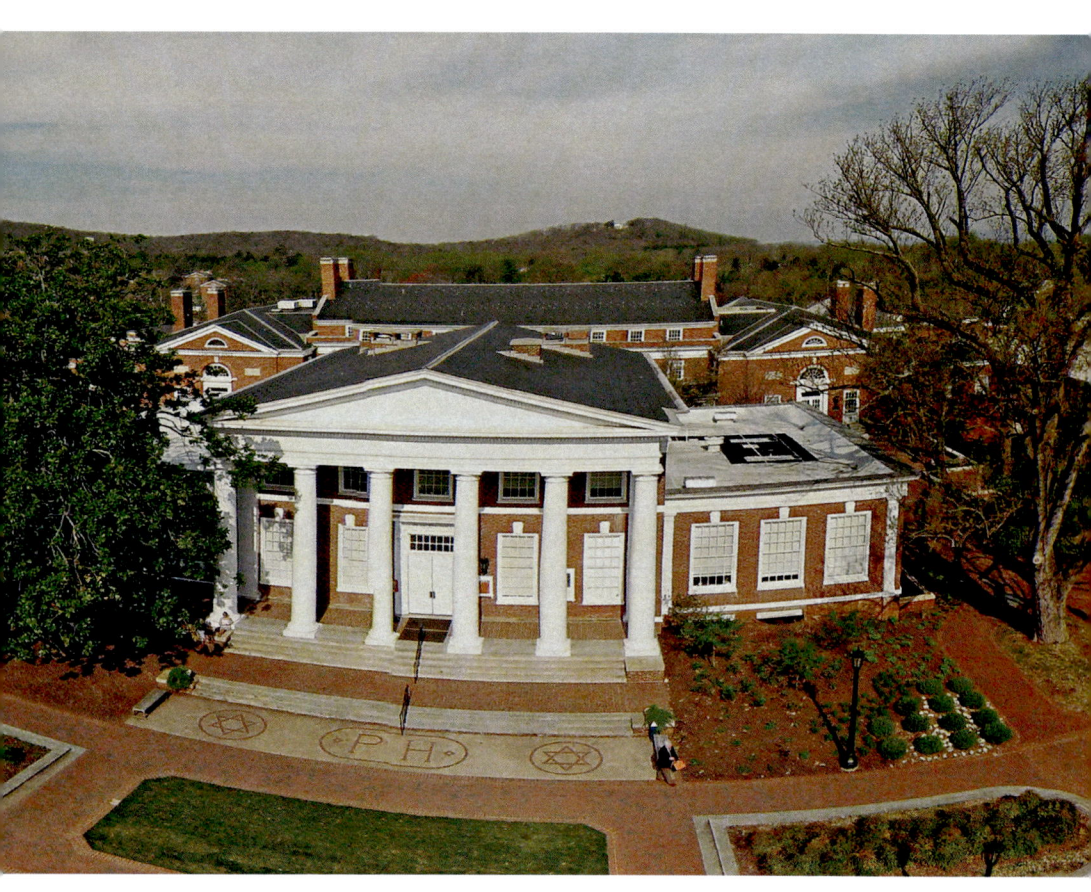

16   Peabody Hall, Harrison Institute, Alderman Library (U.Va.)

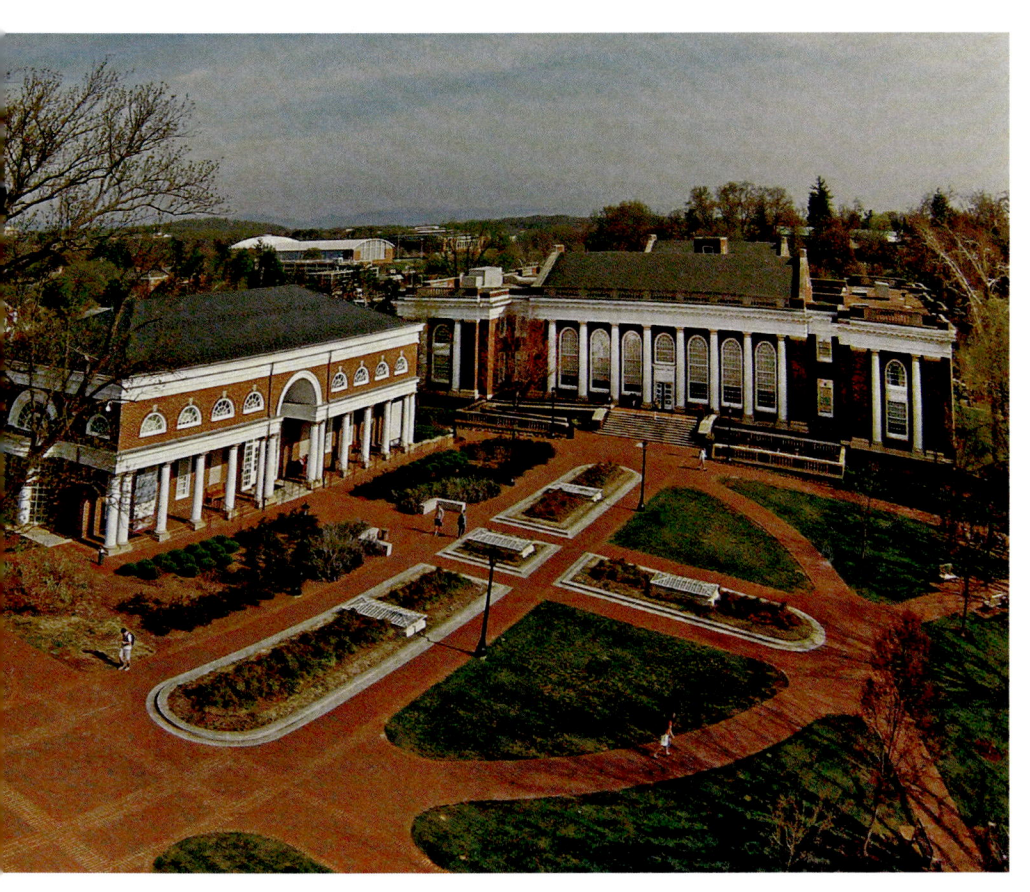

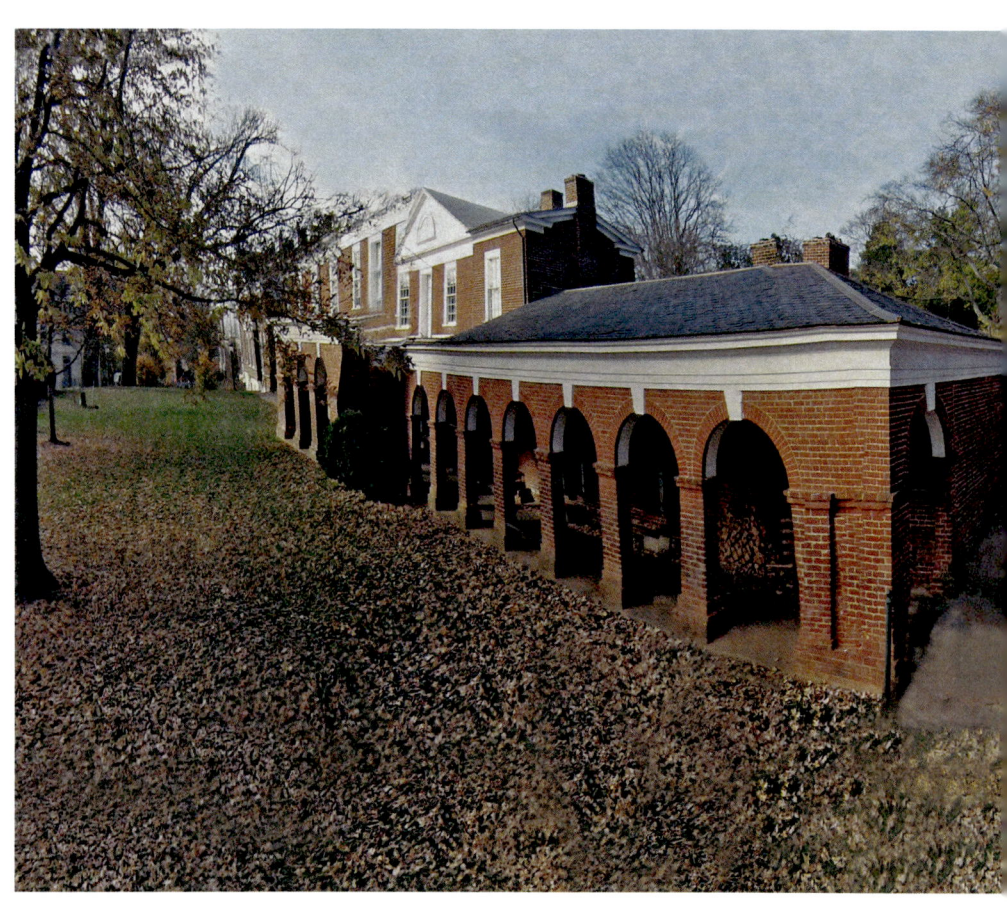

18   East Range at Lile Alley (U.Va.)

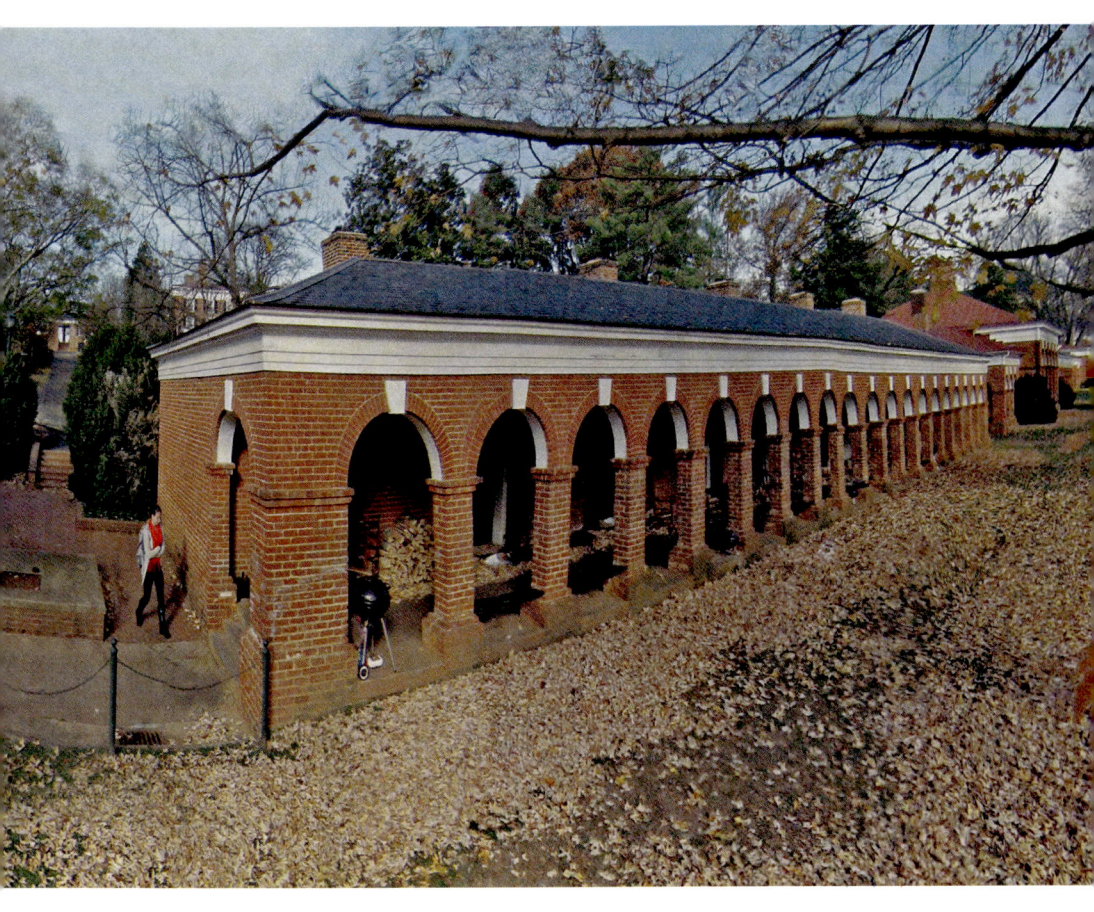

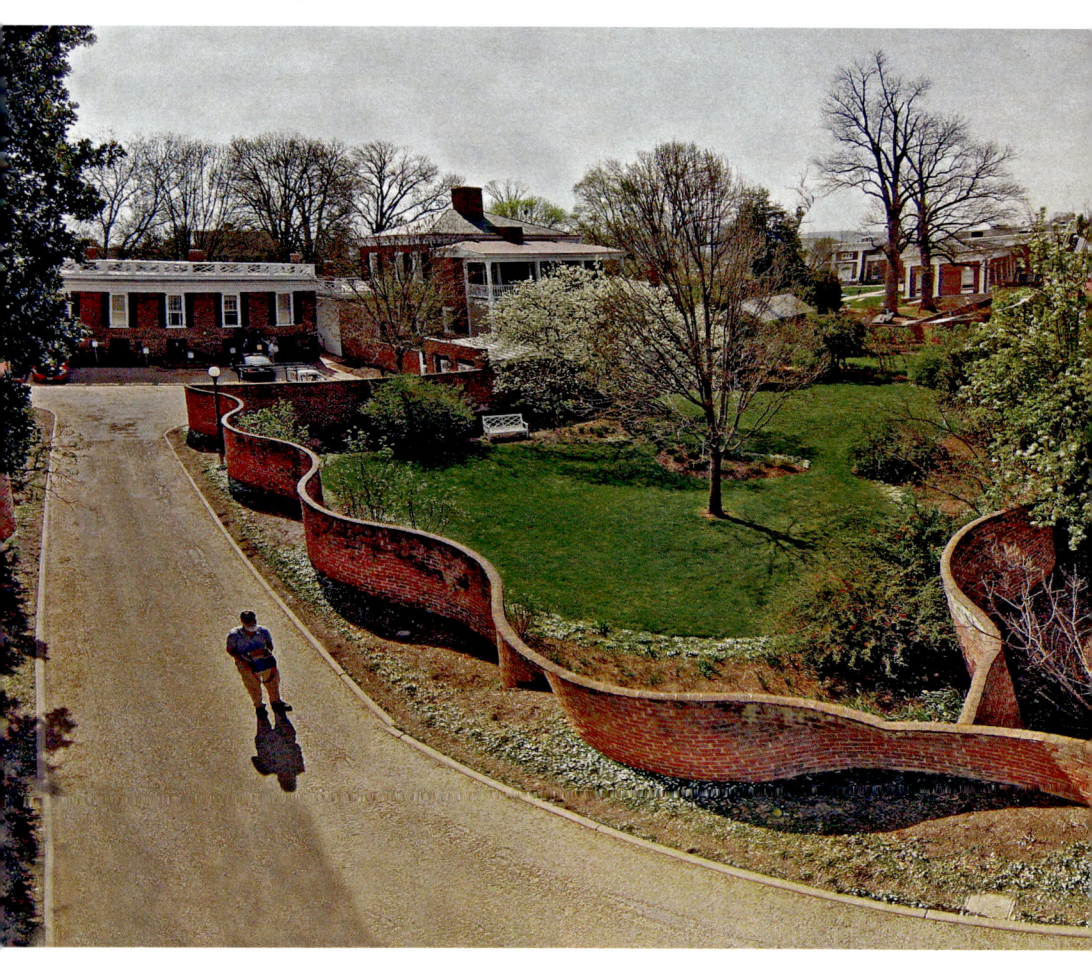

20 Pavilion IX garden (U.Va.)

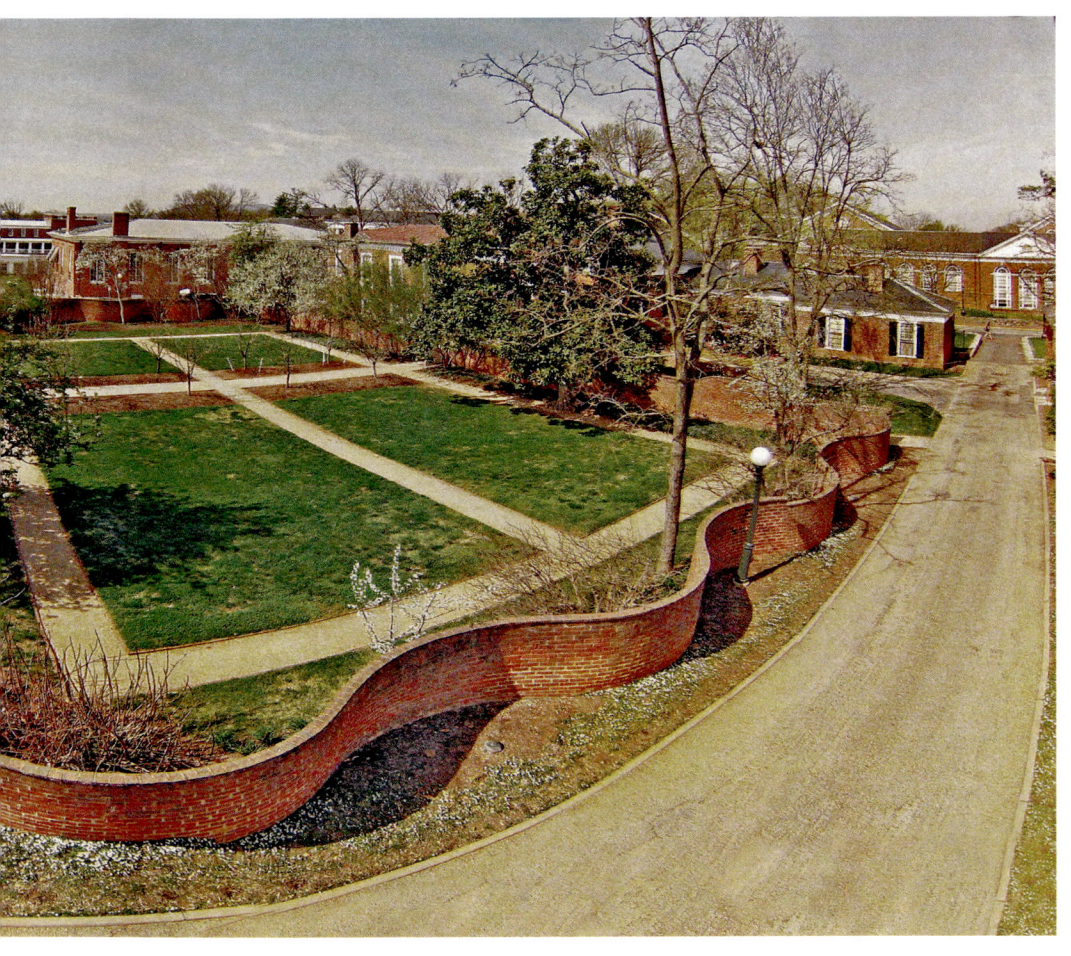

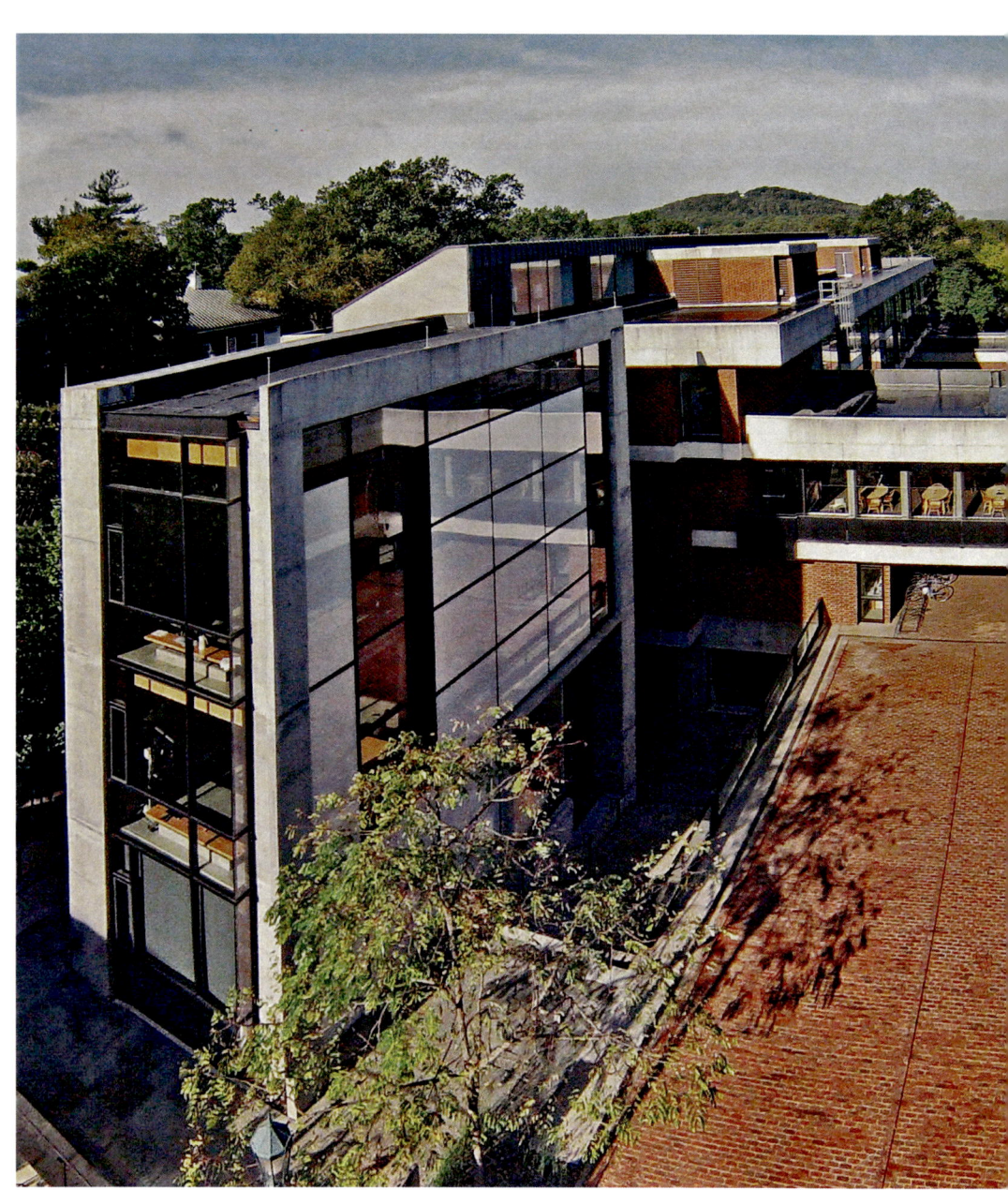

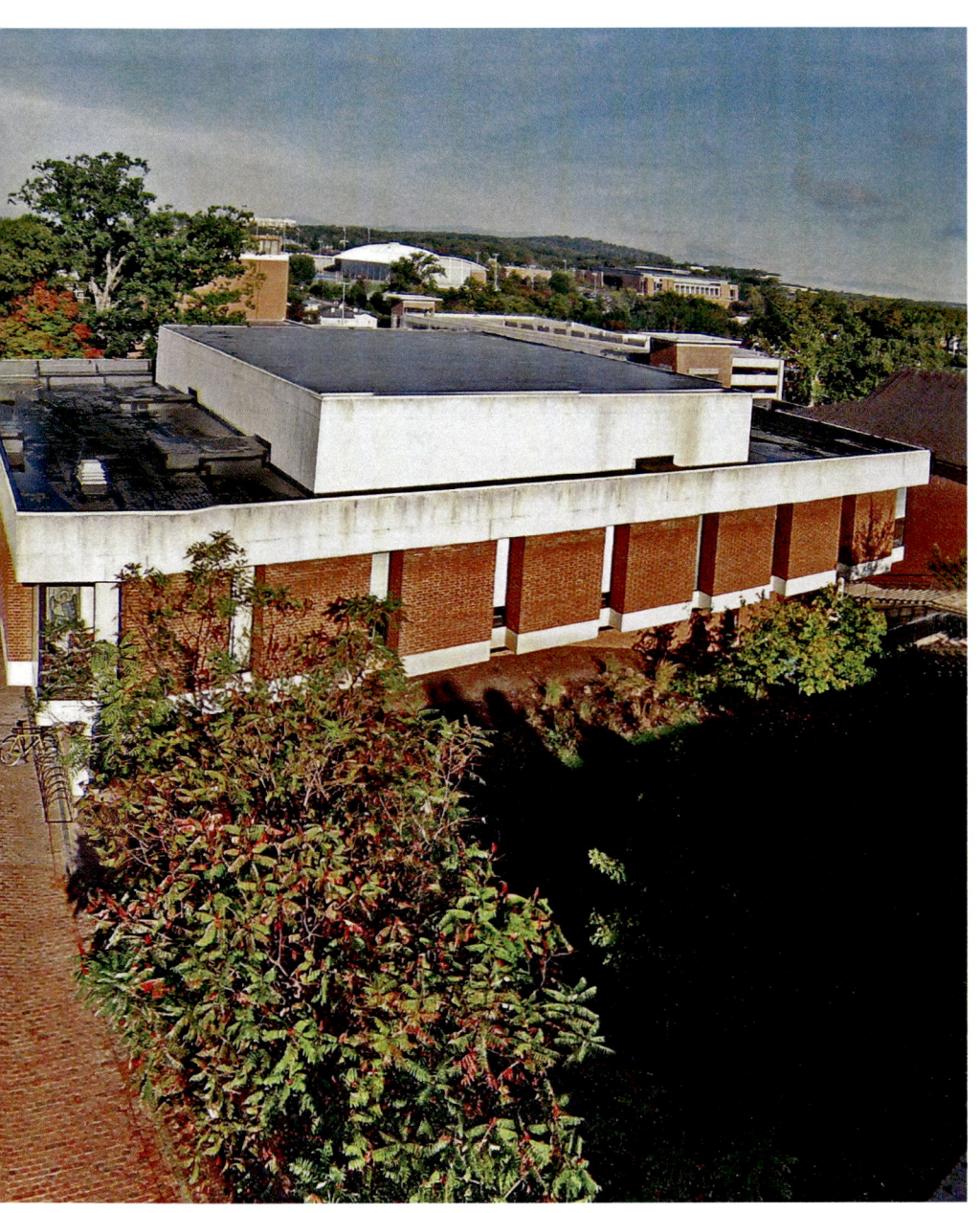

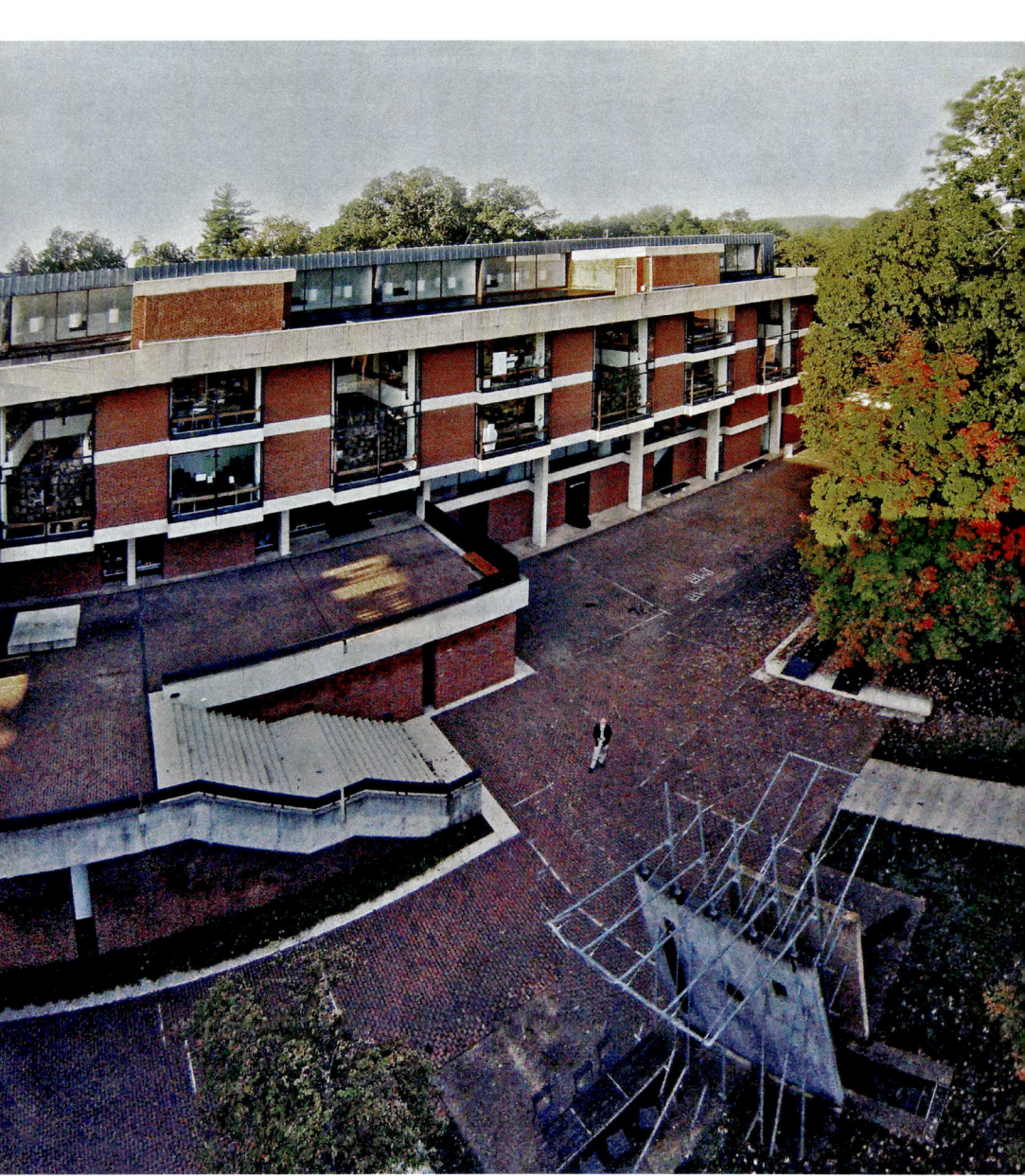

24   Campbell Hall and Caplin Theater (U.Va.)

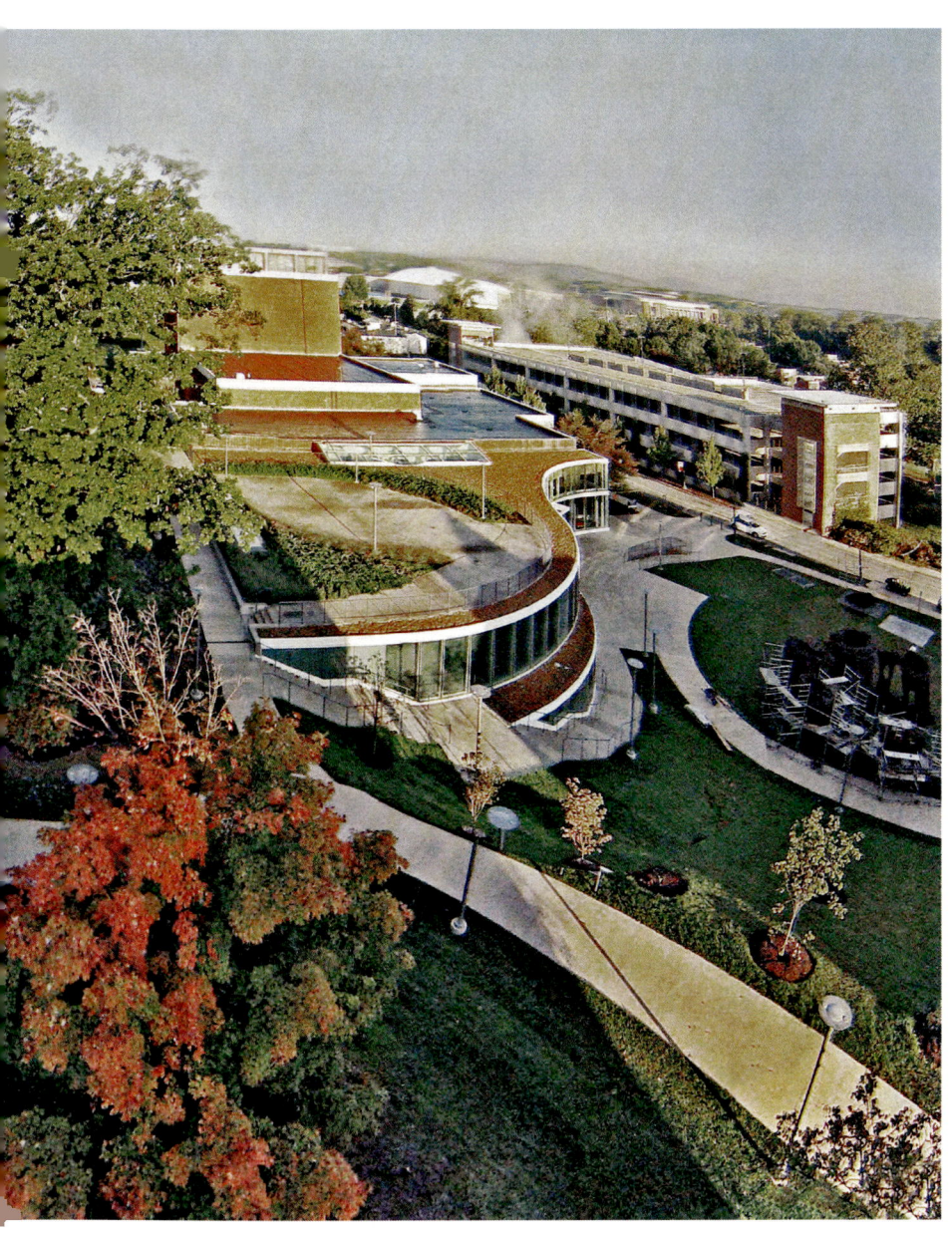

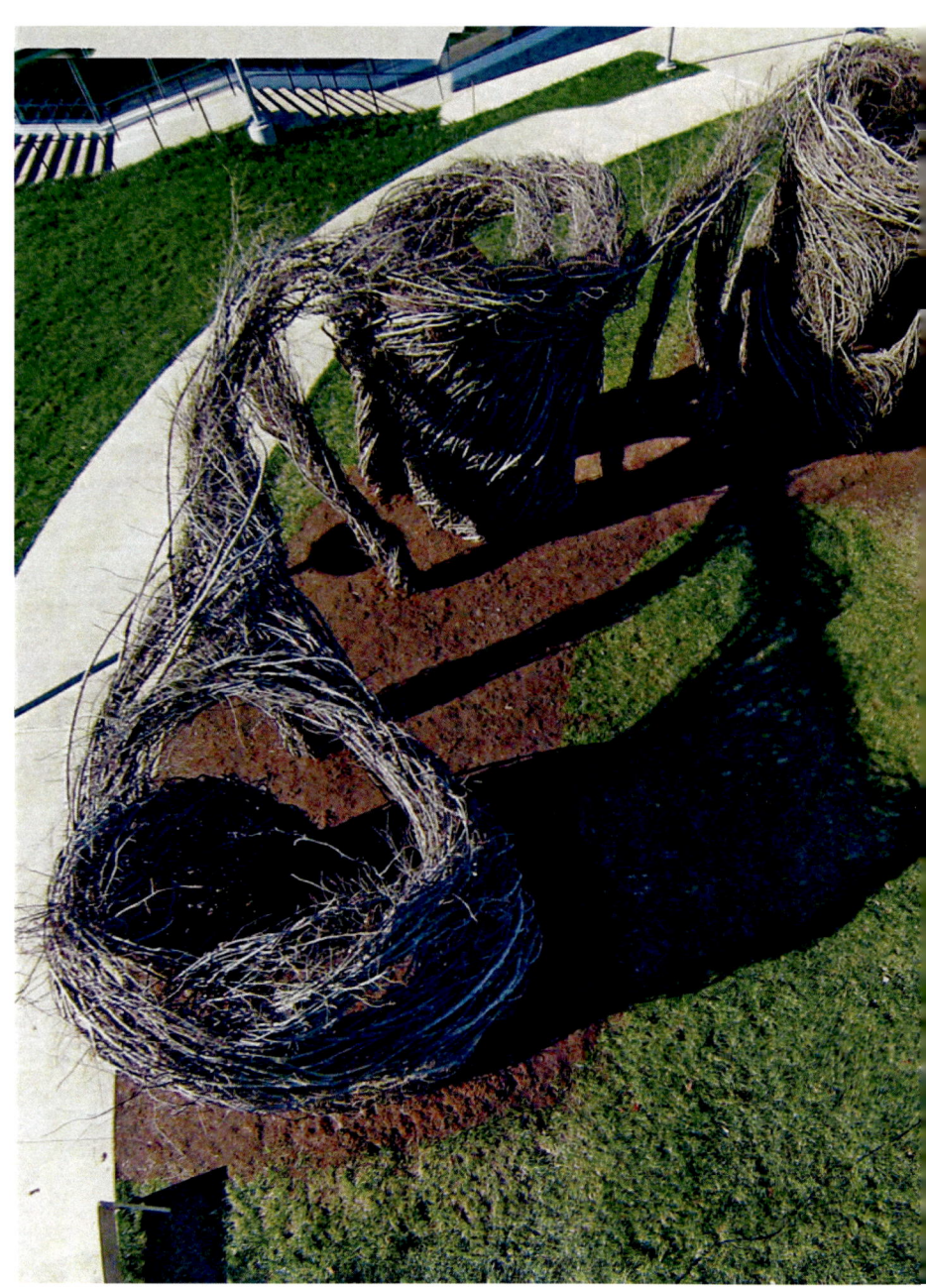

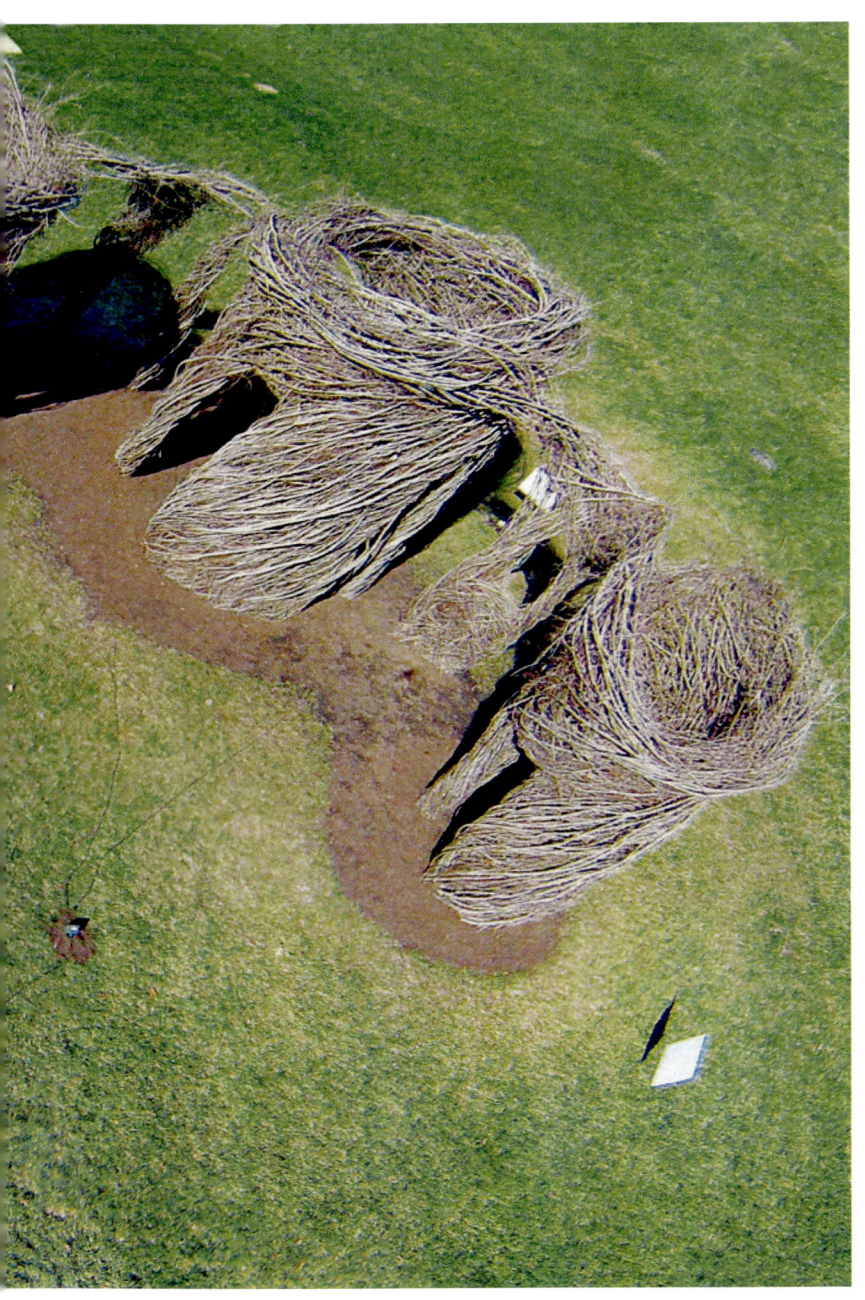

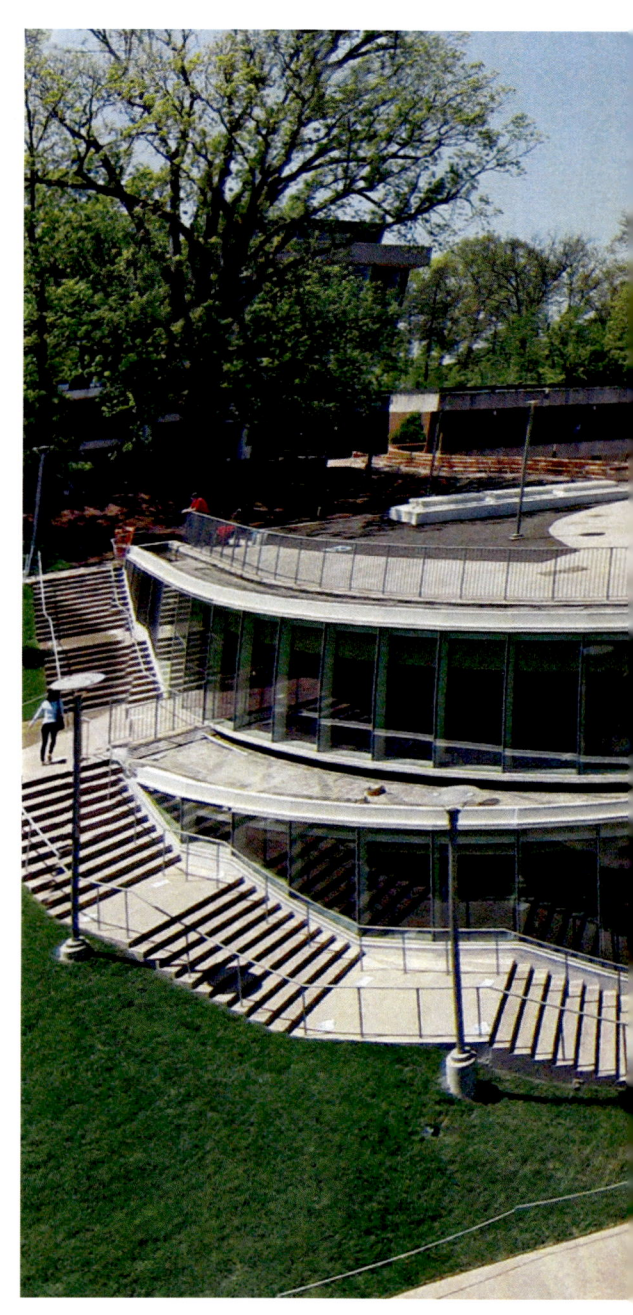

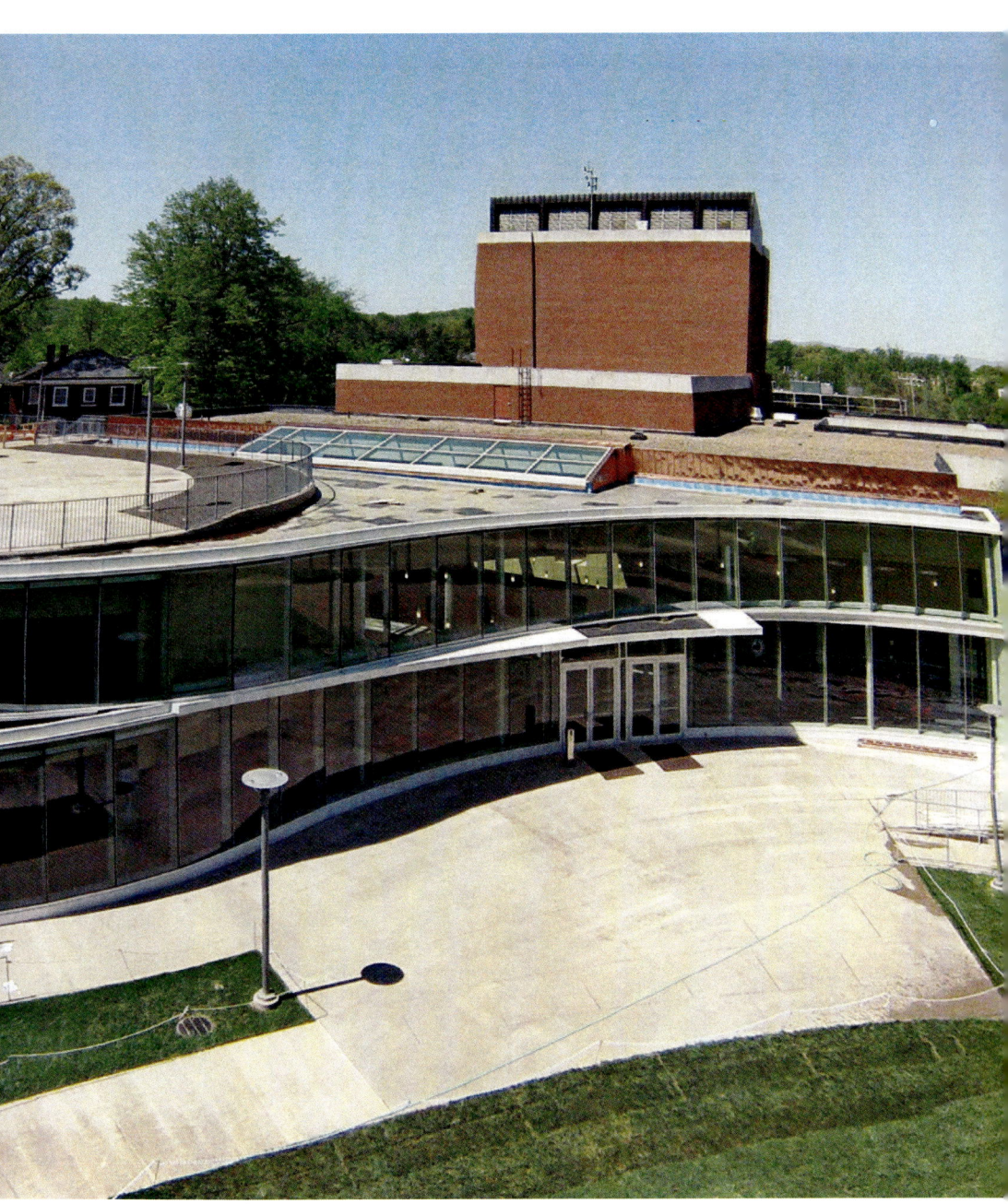

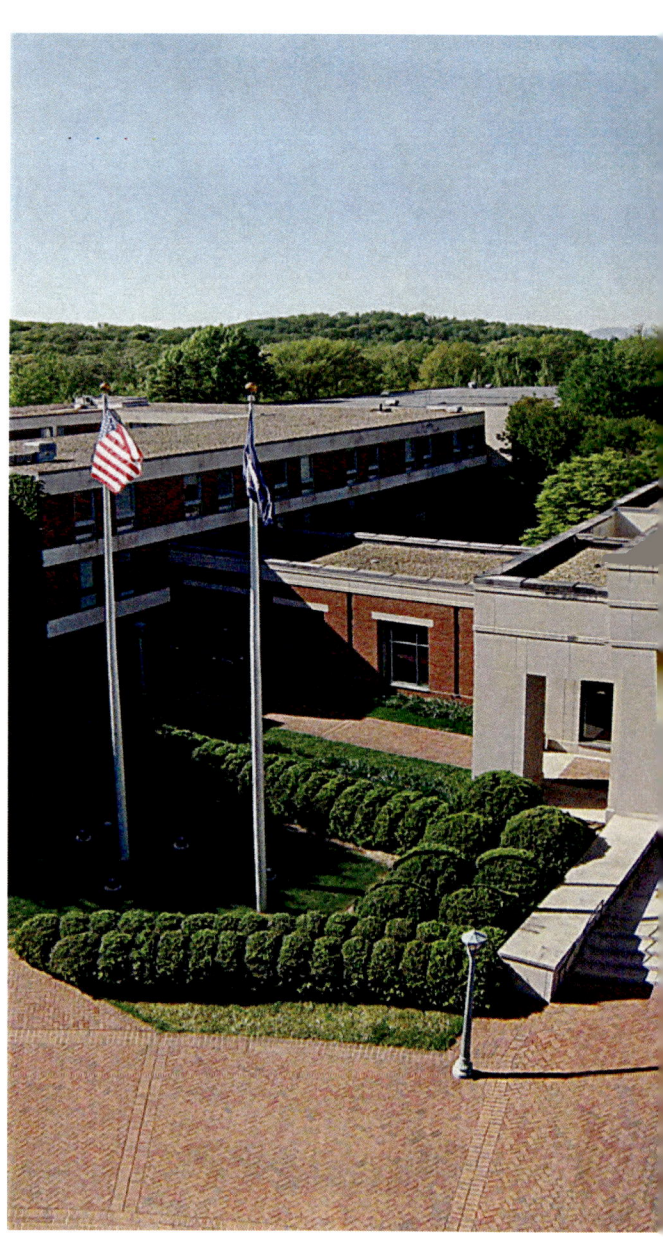

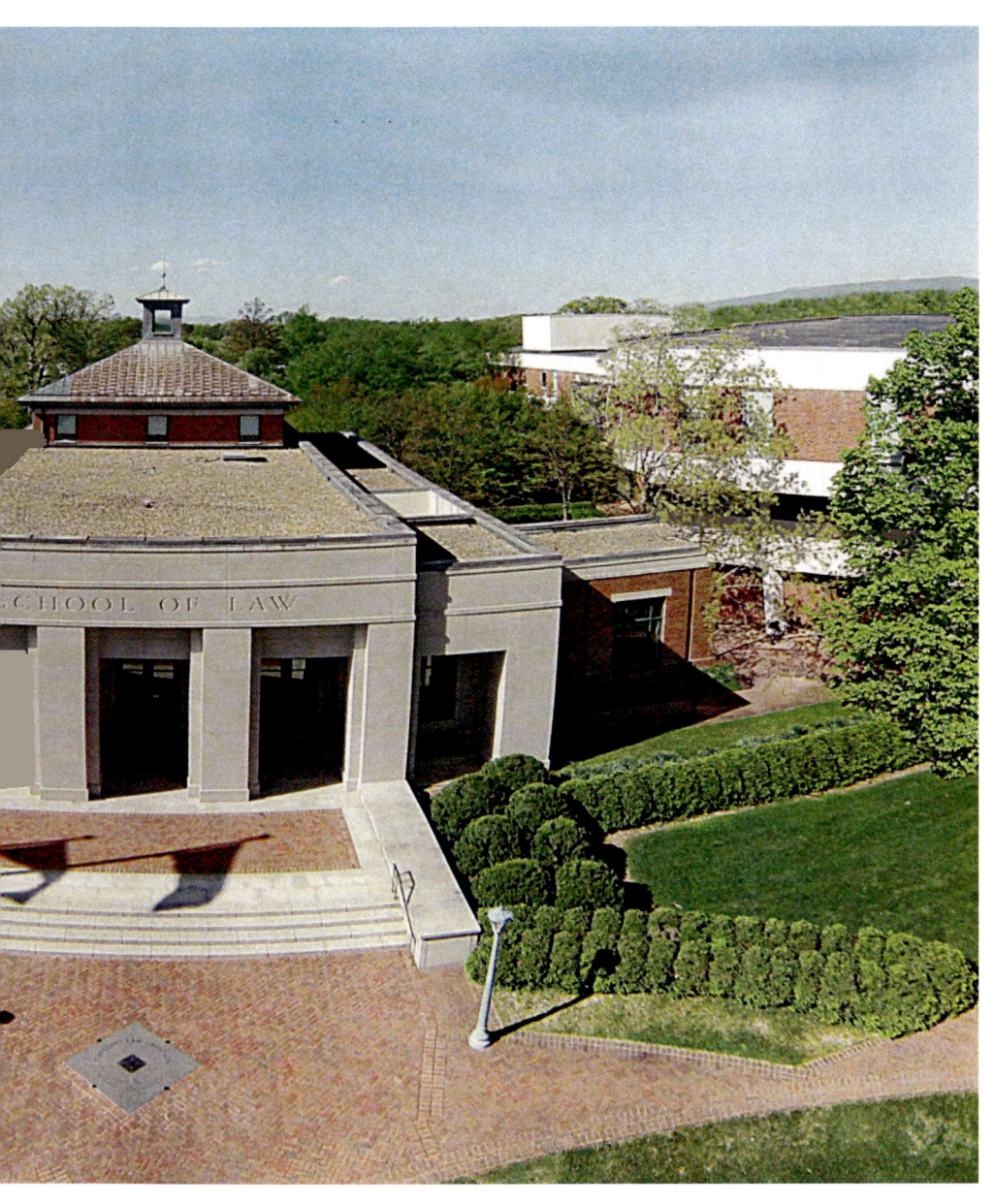

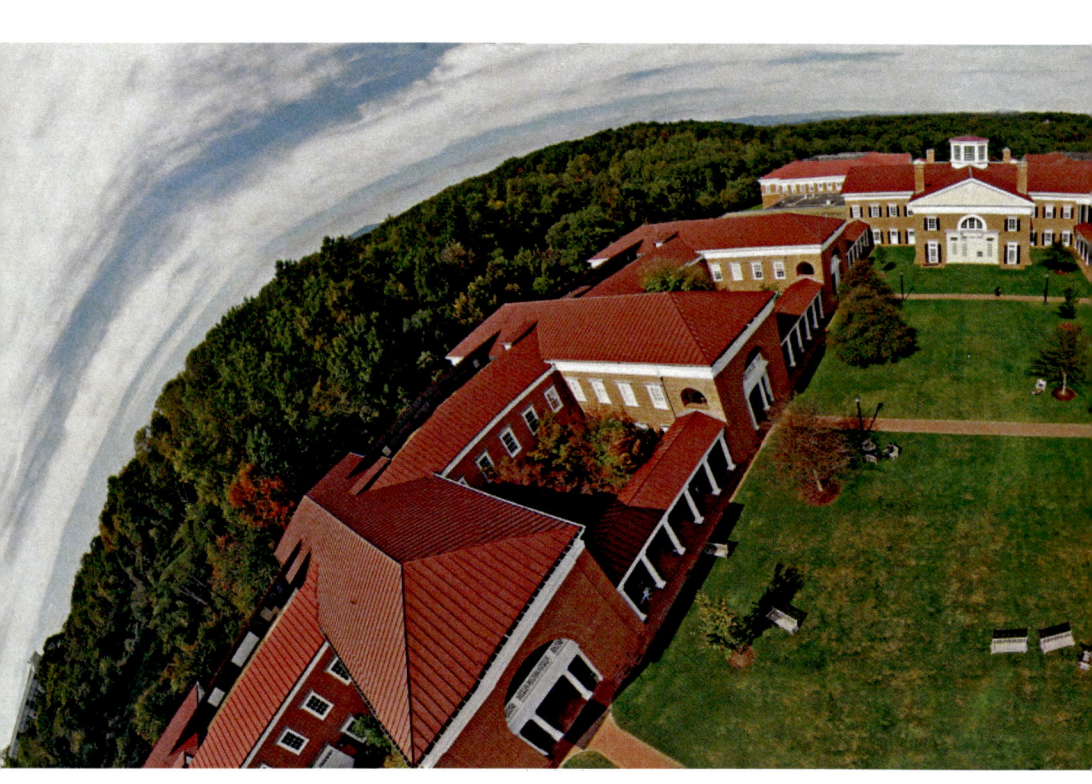

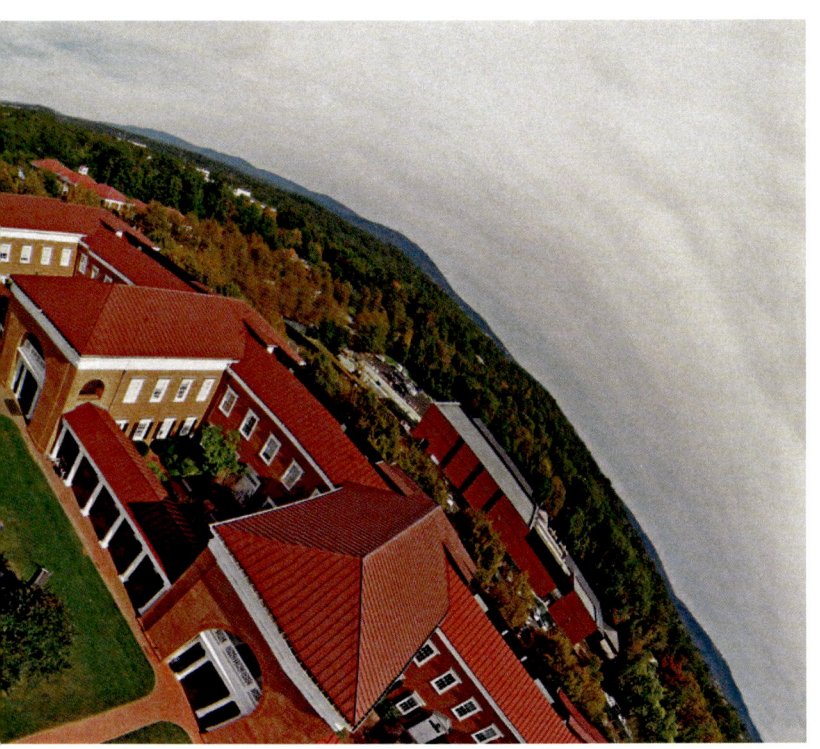

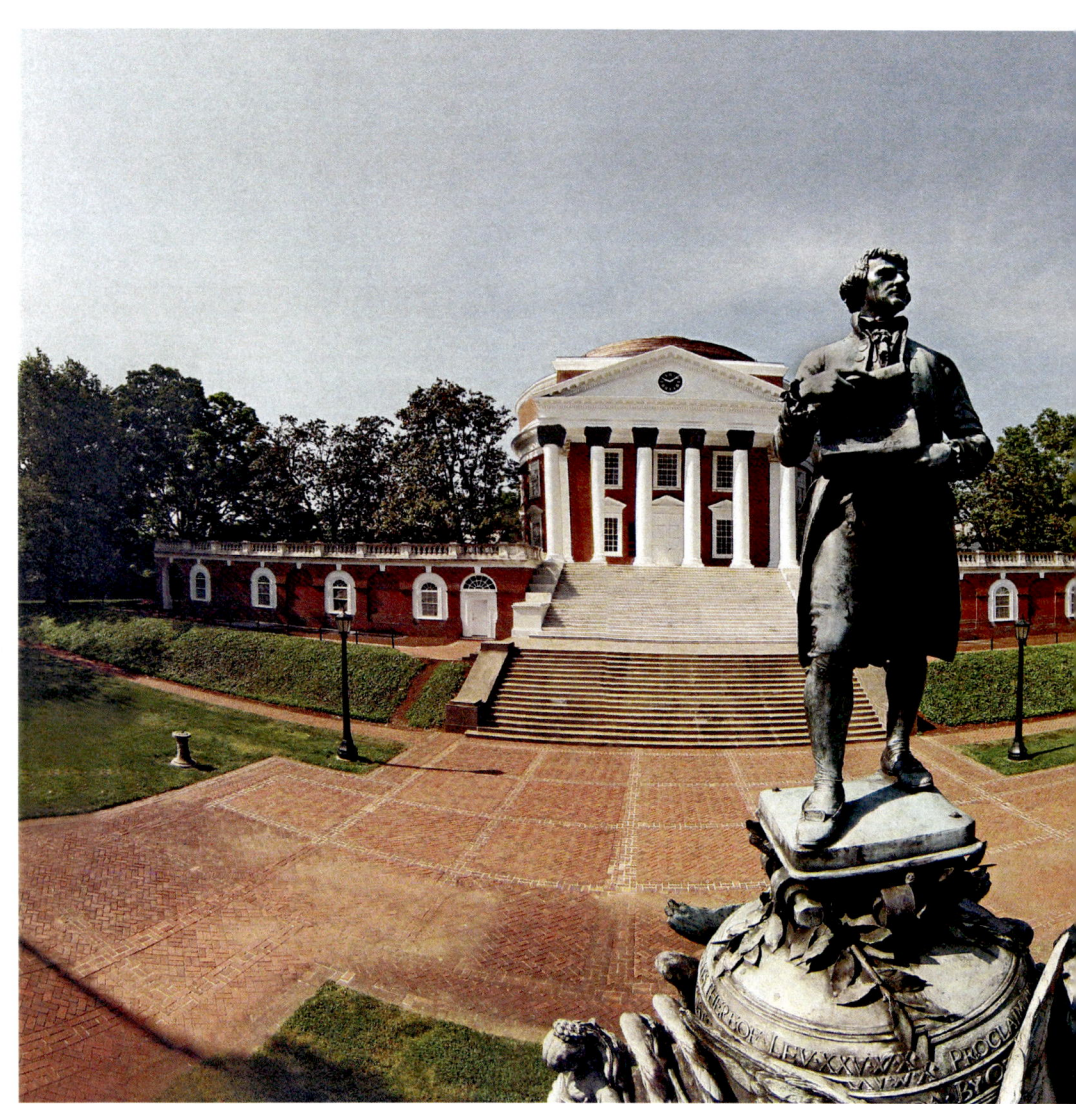

34   Thomas Jefferson statue and Rotunda (U.Va.)

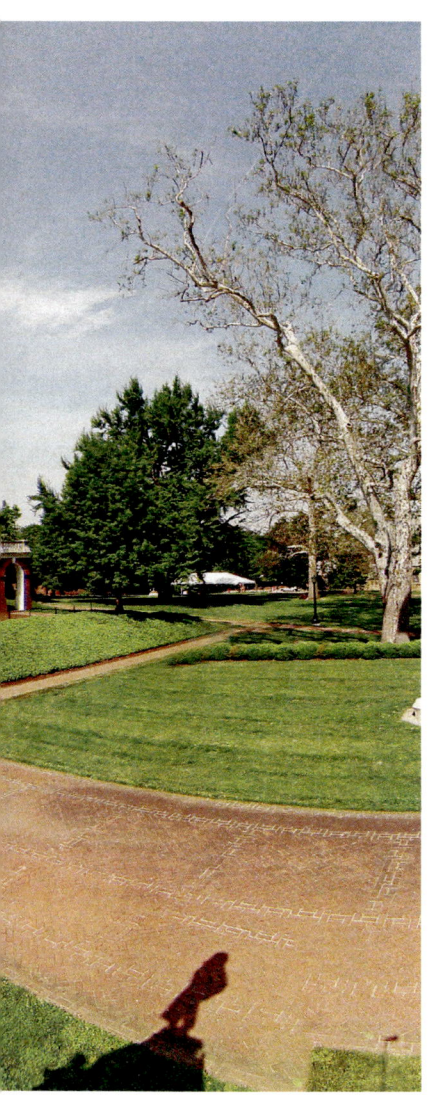

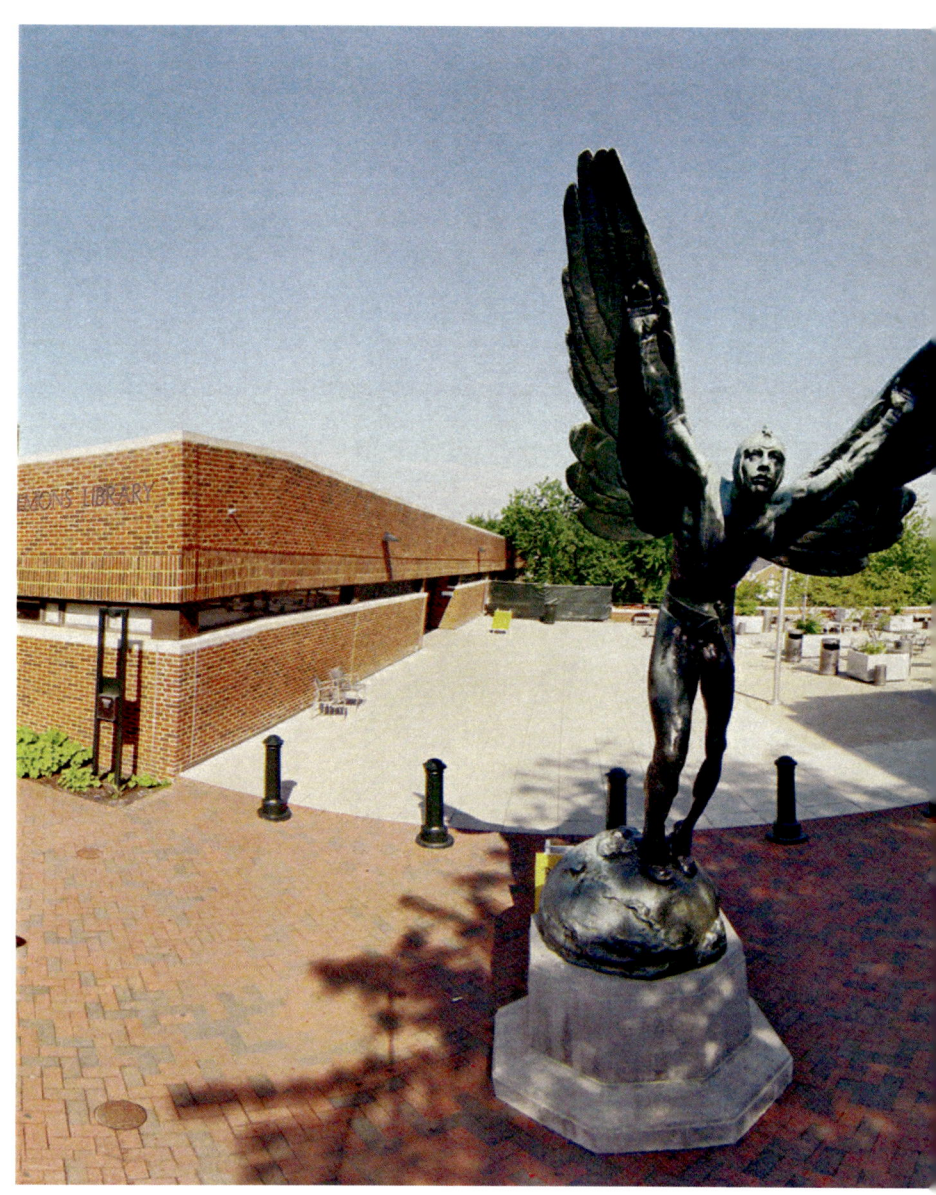

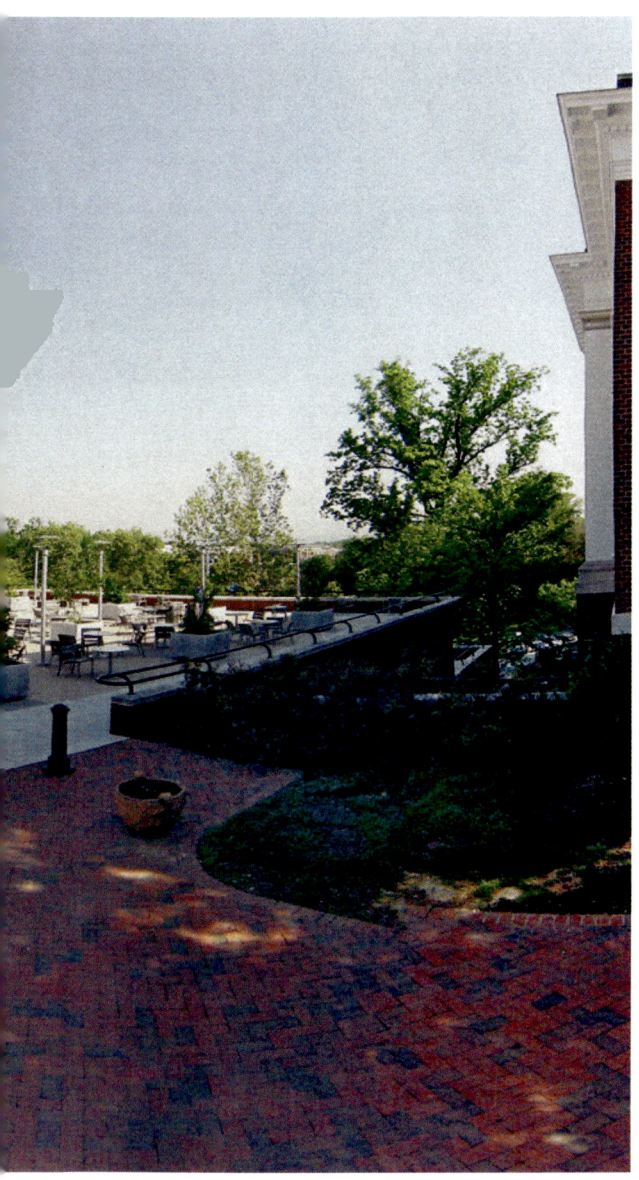

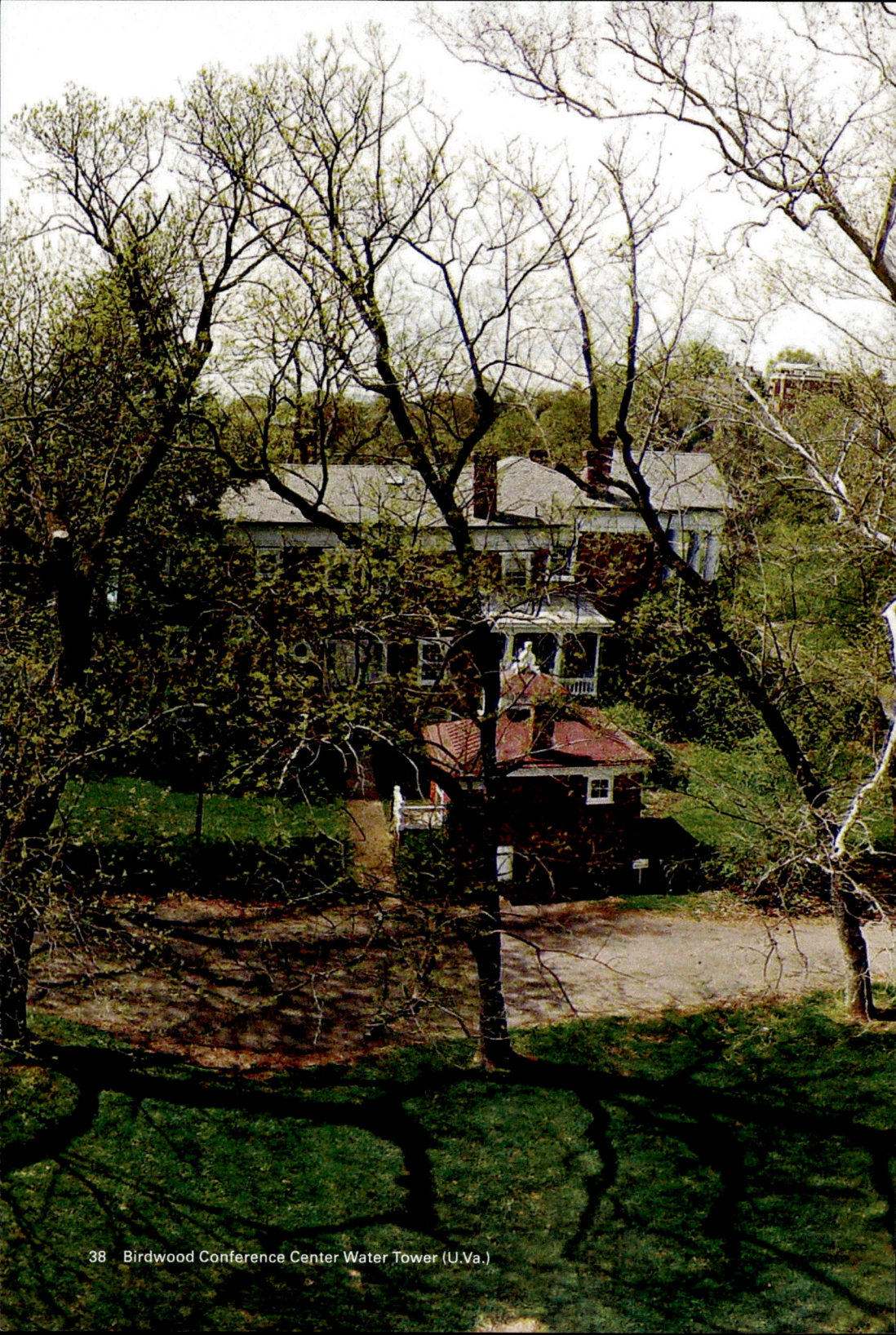

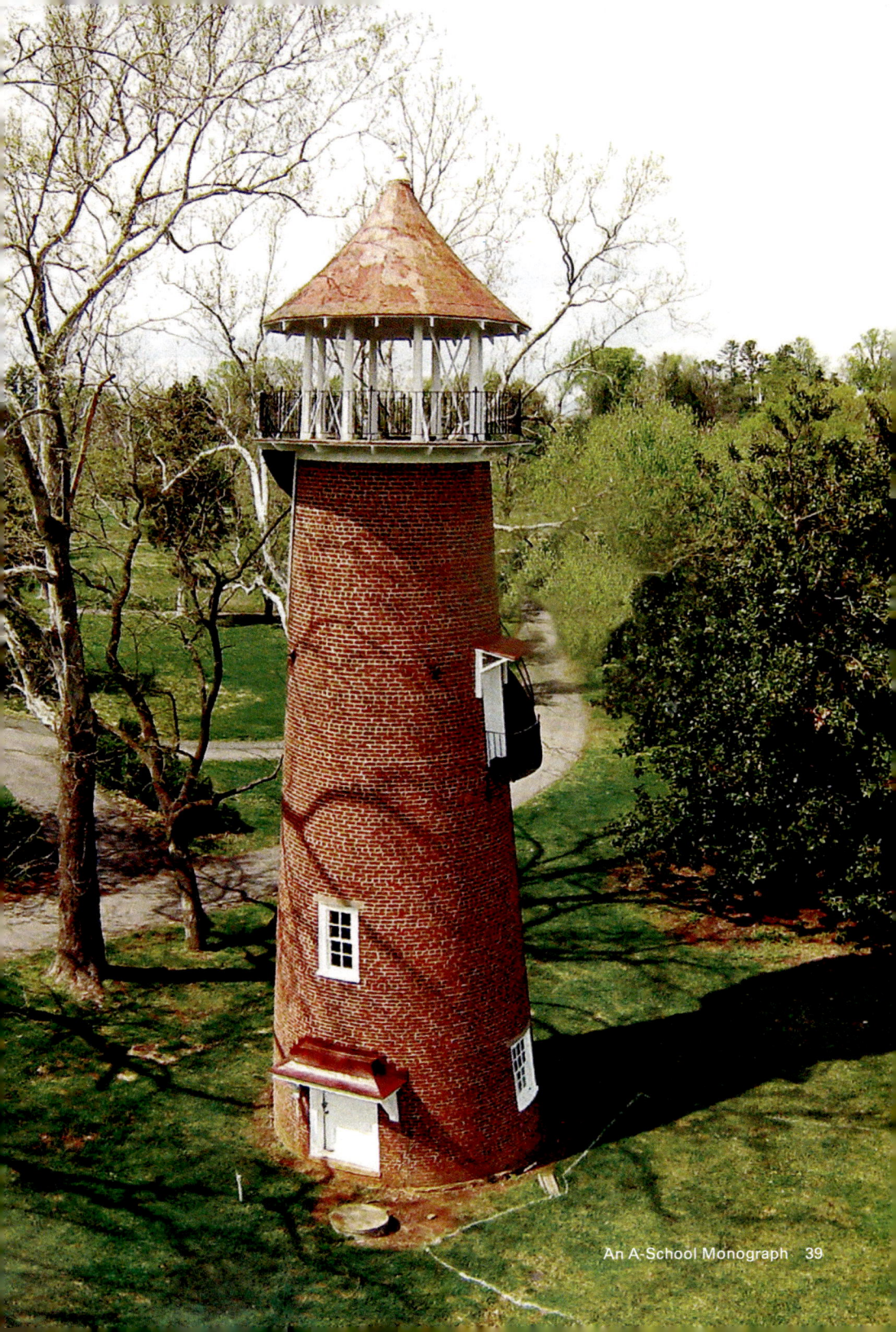

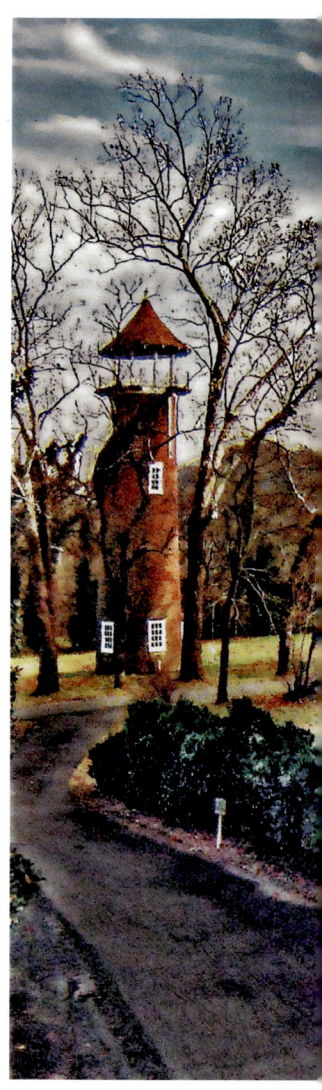

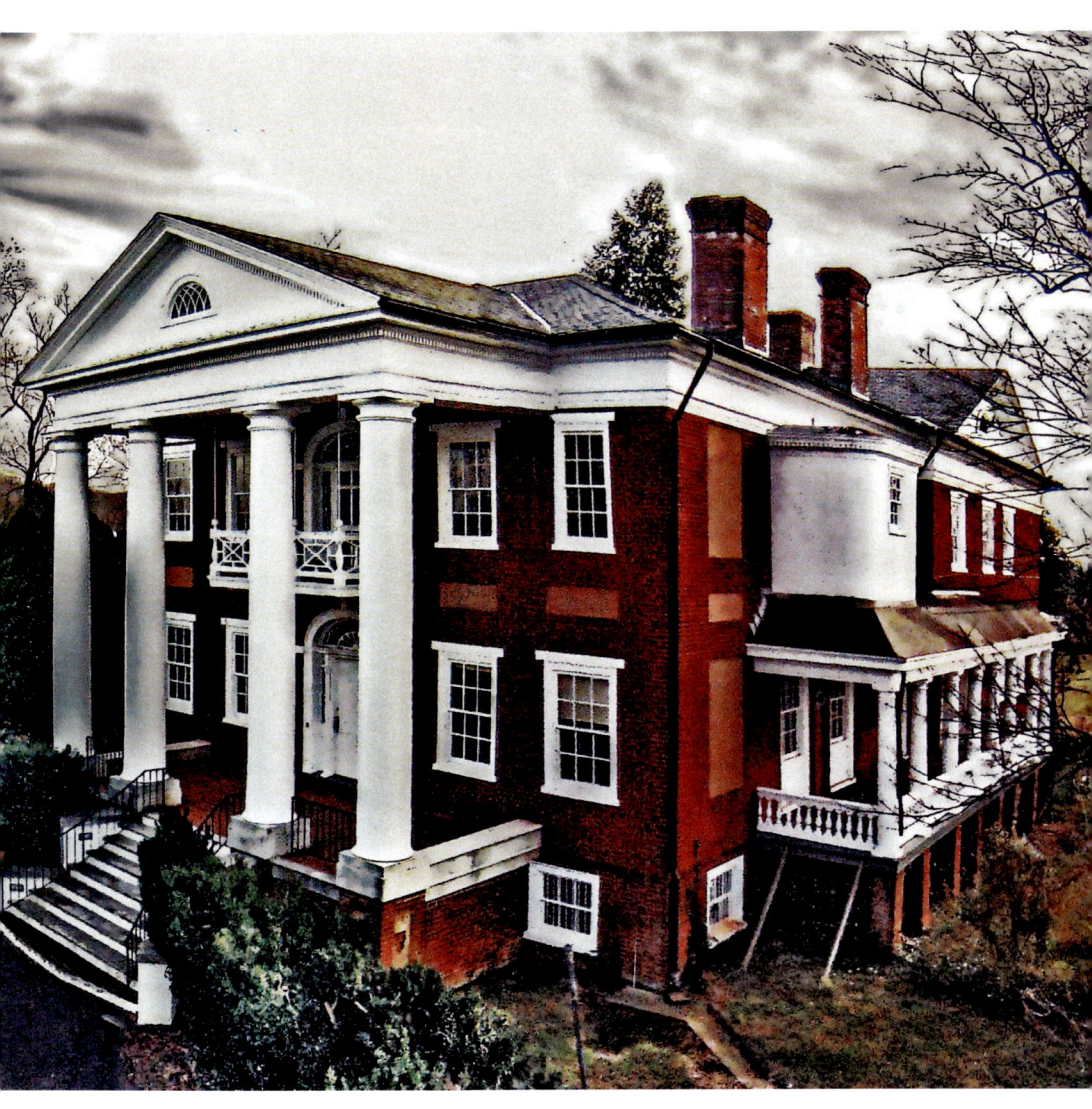

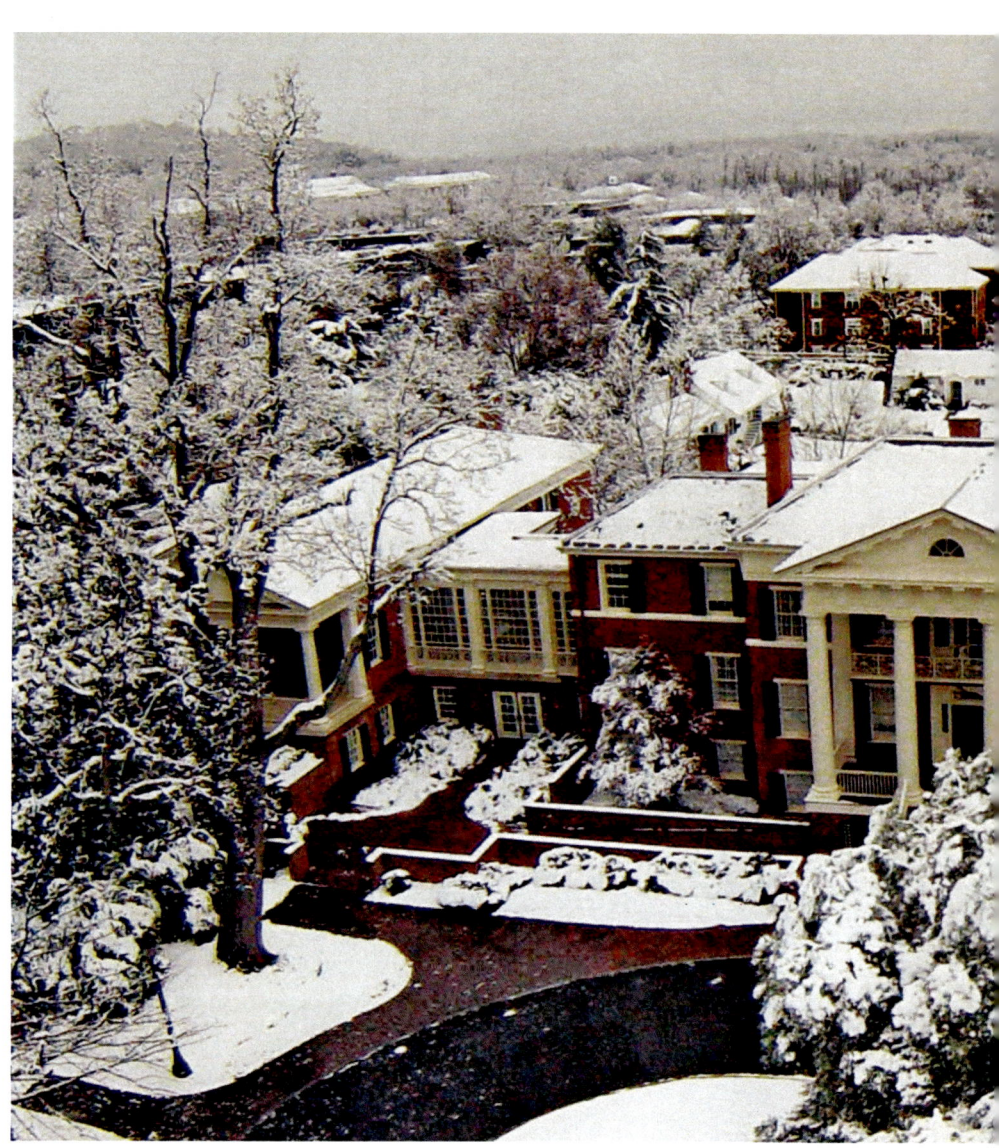

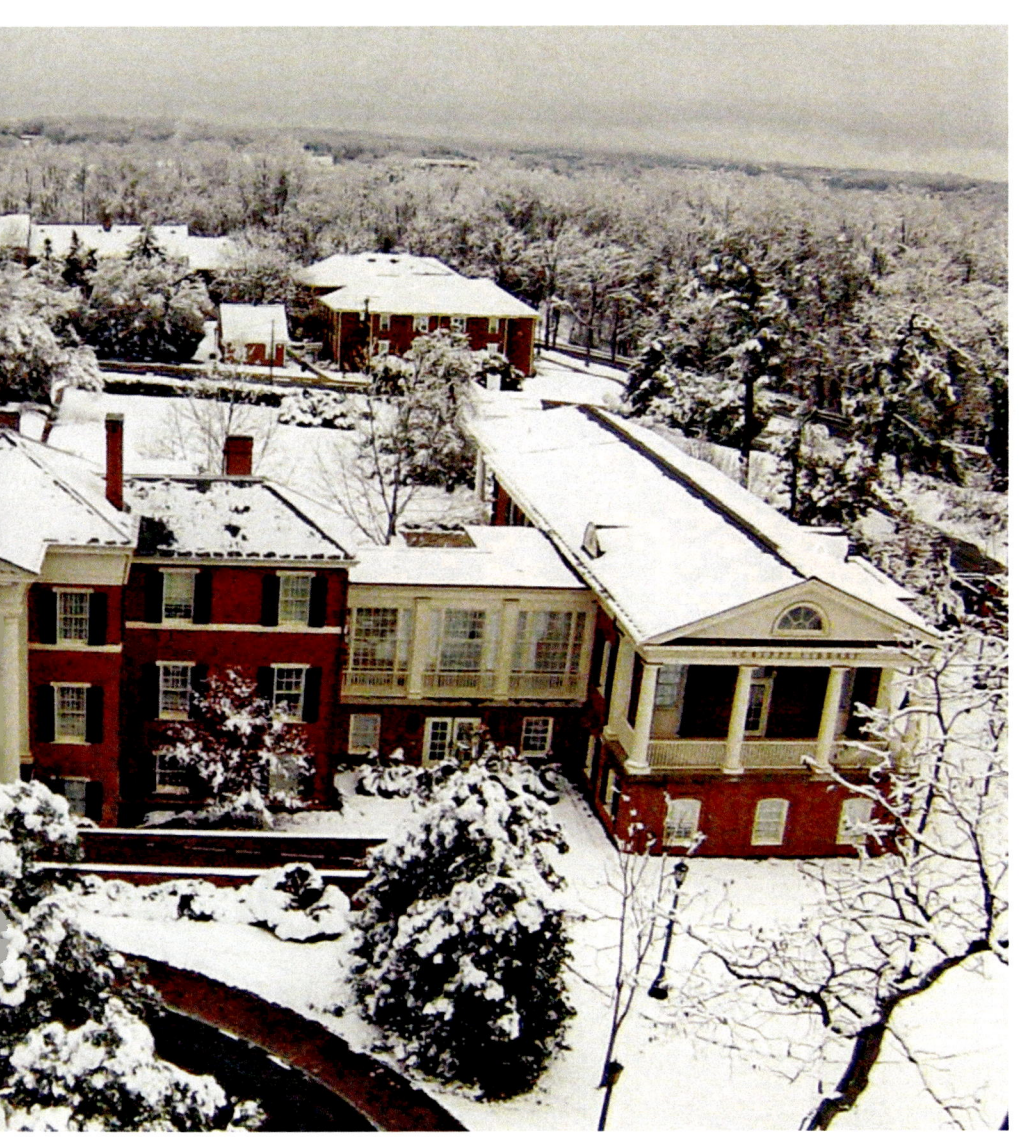

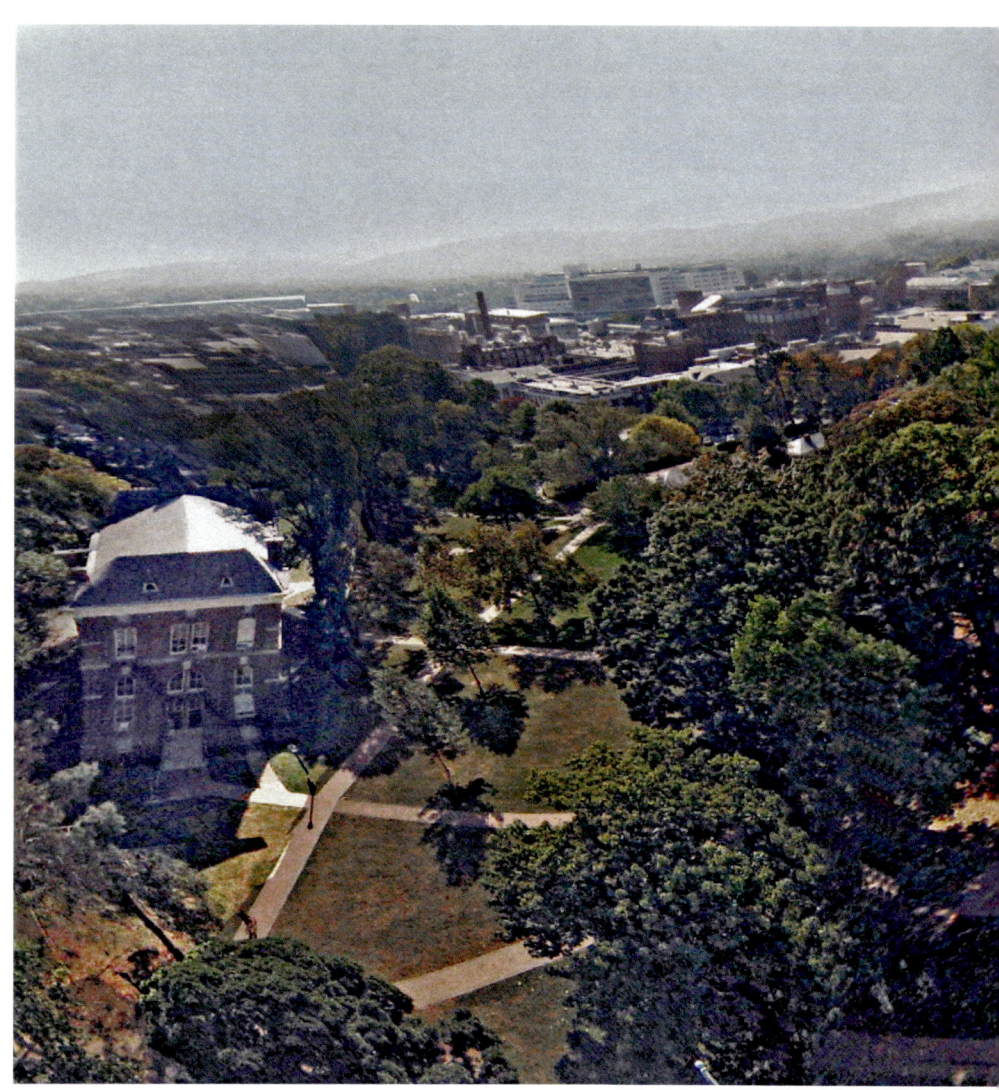

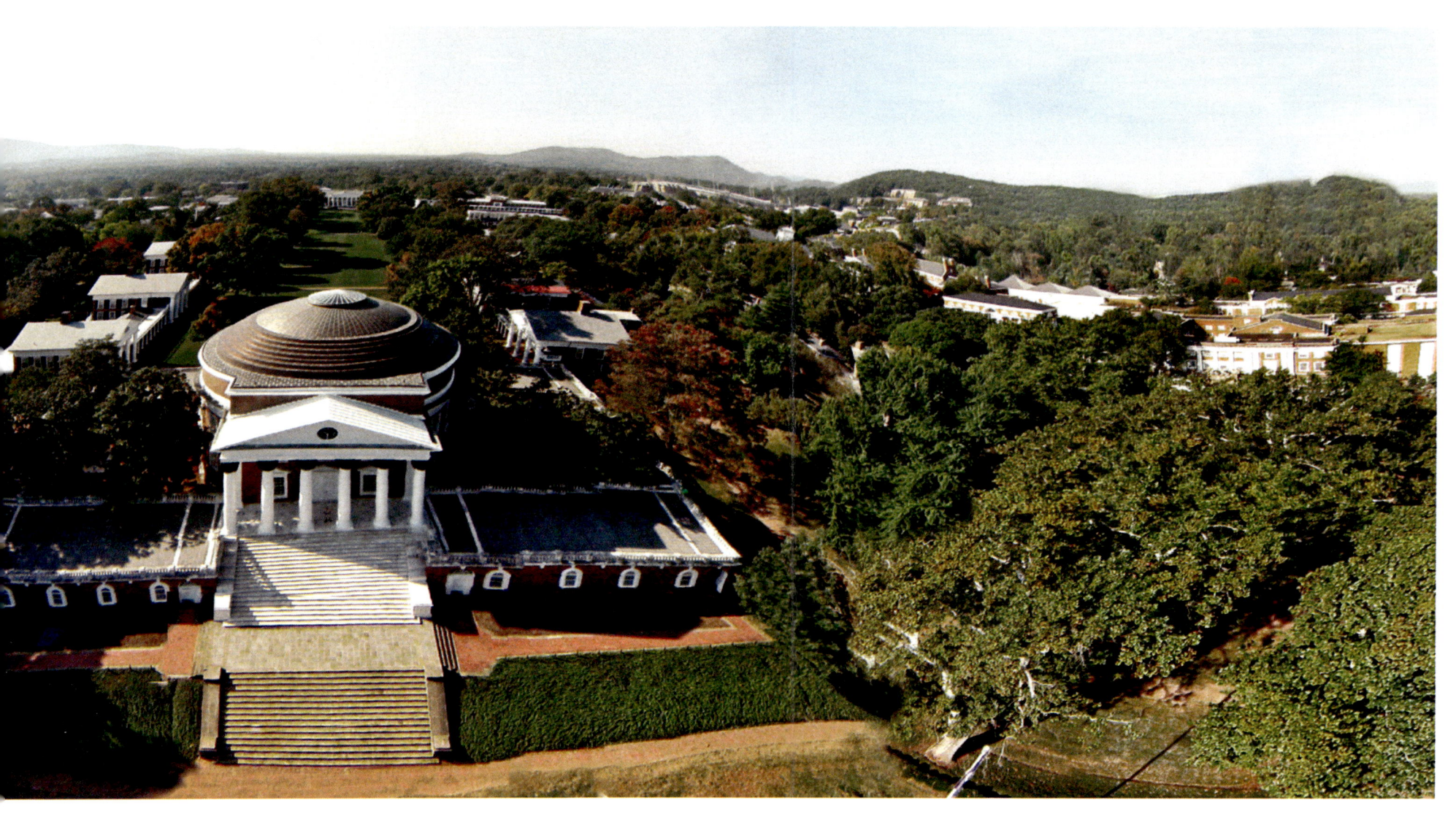

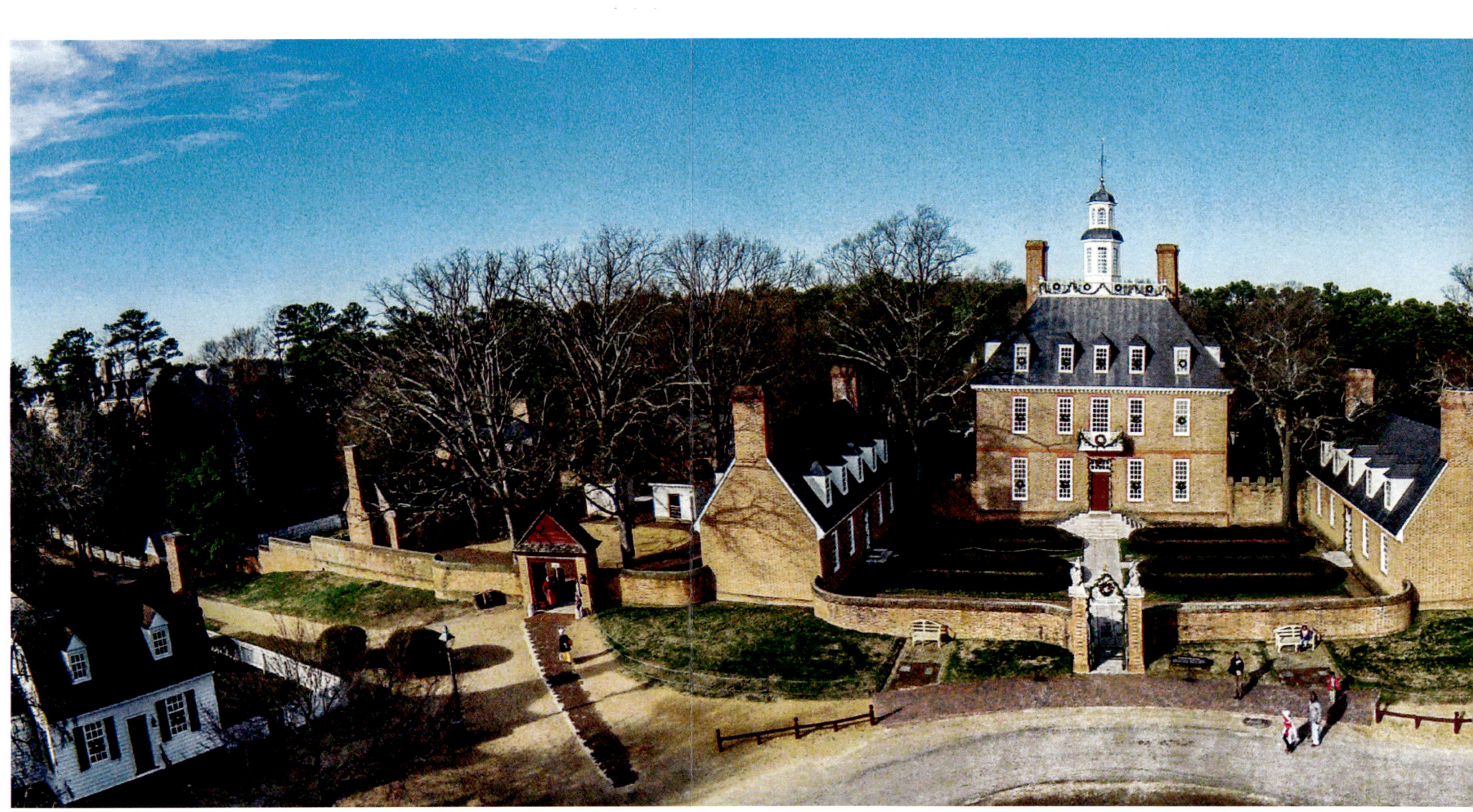

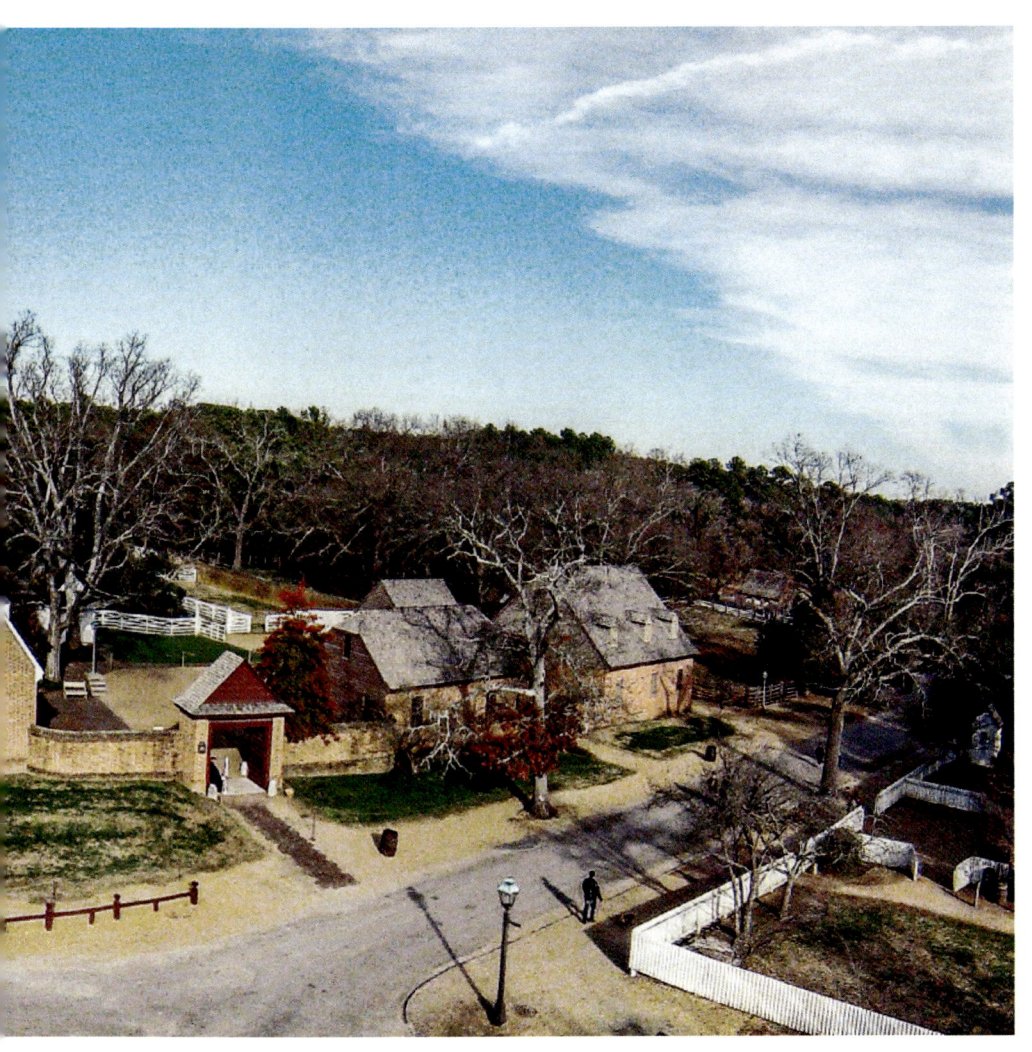

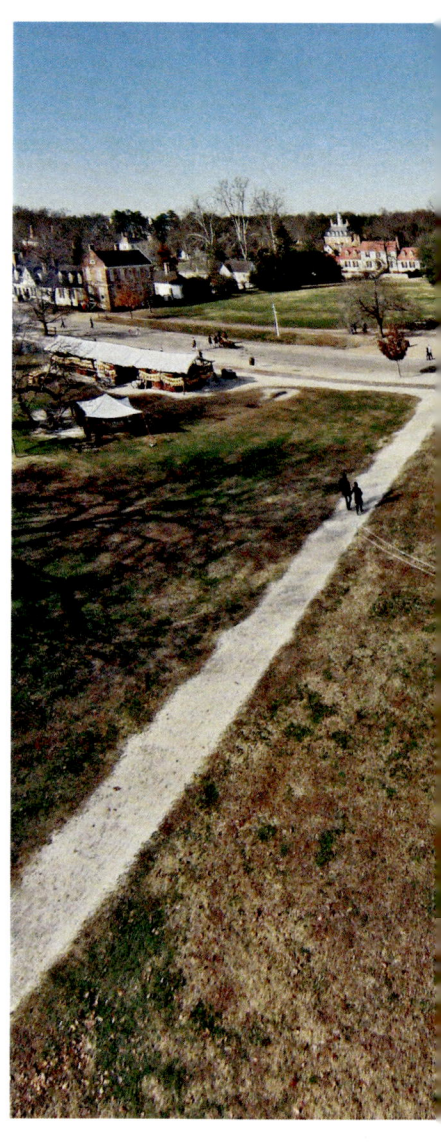

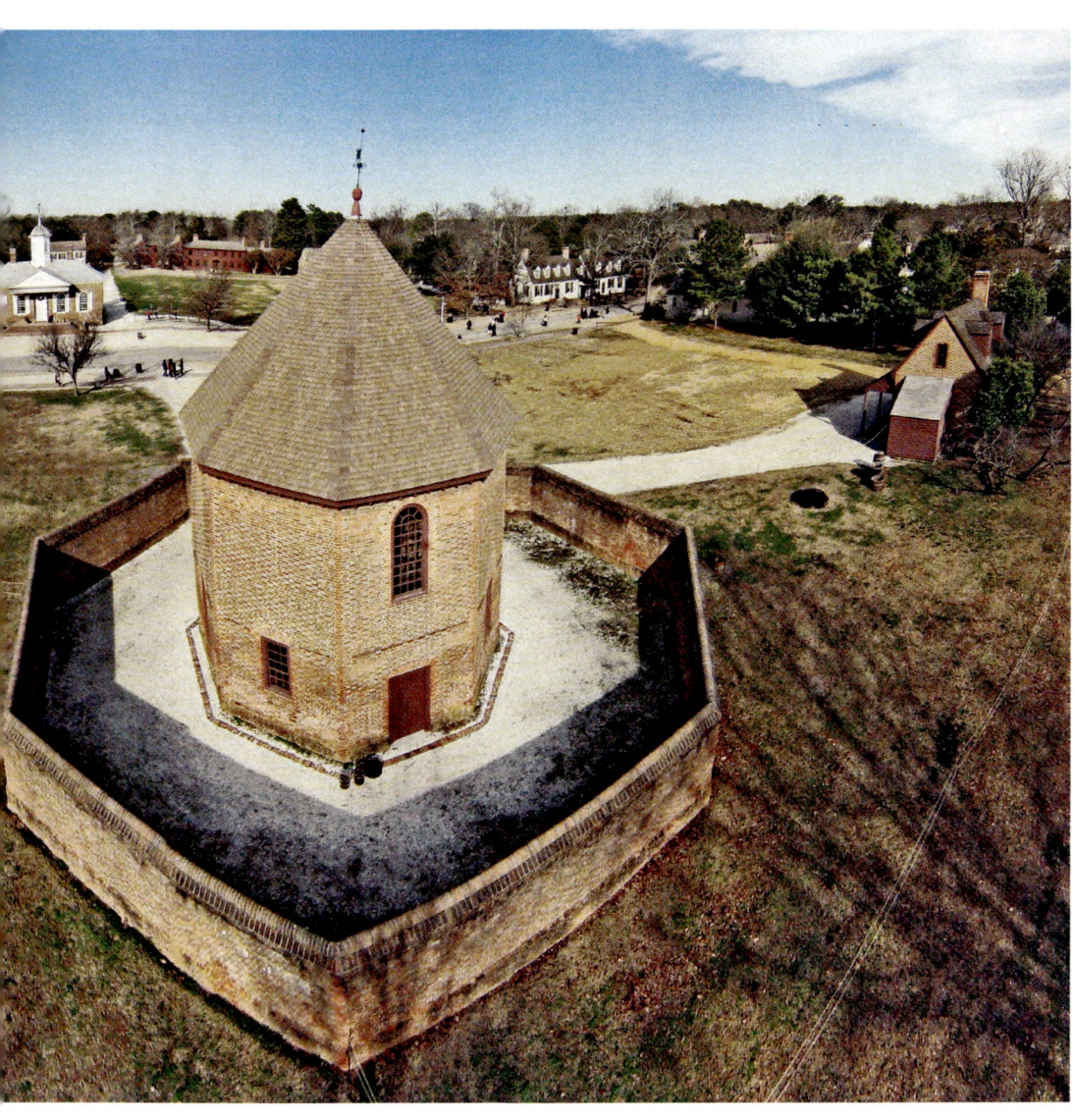

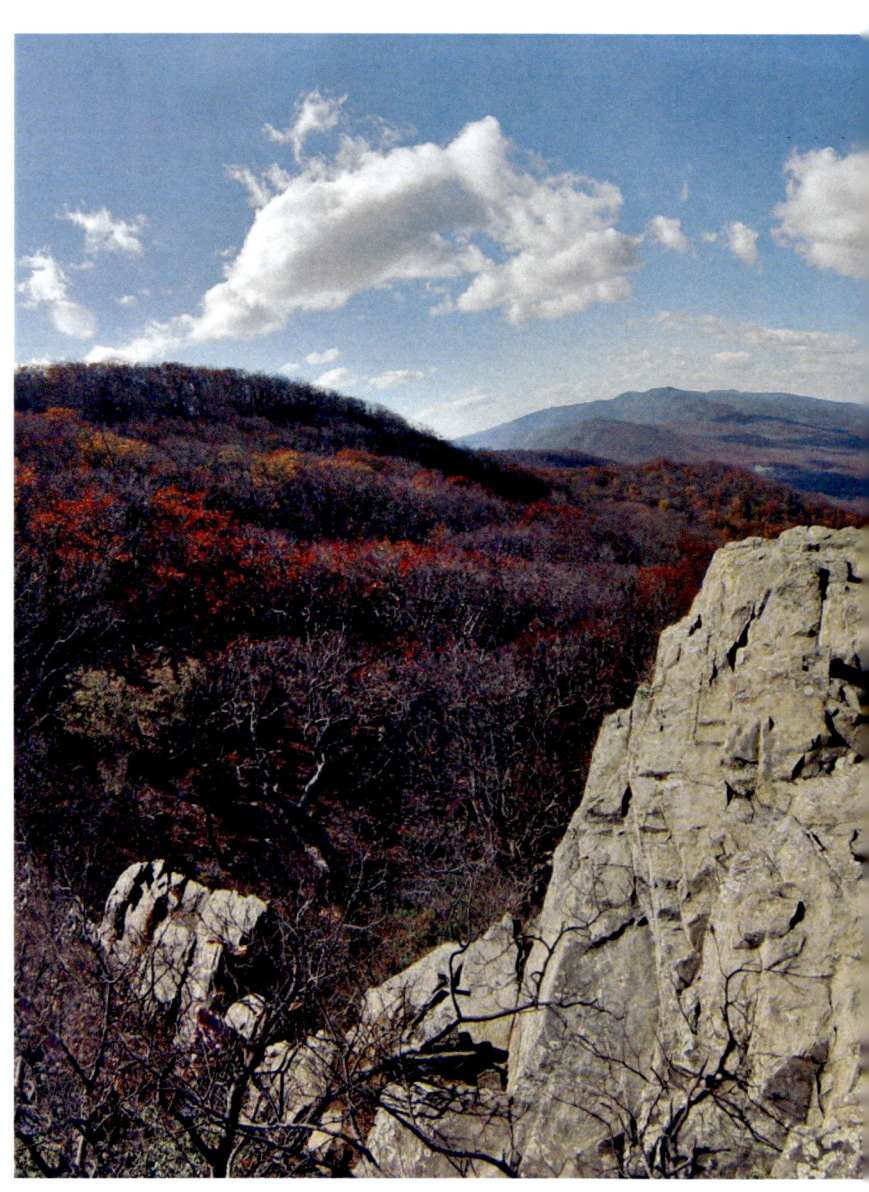

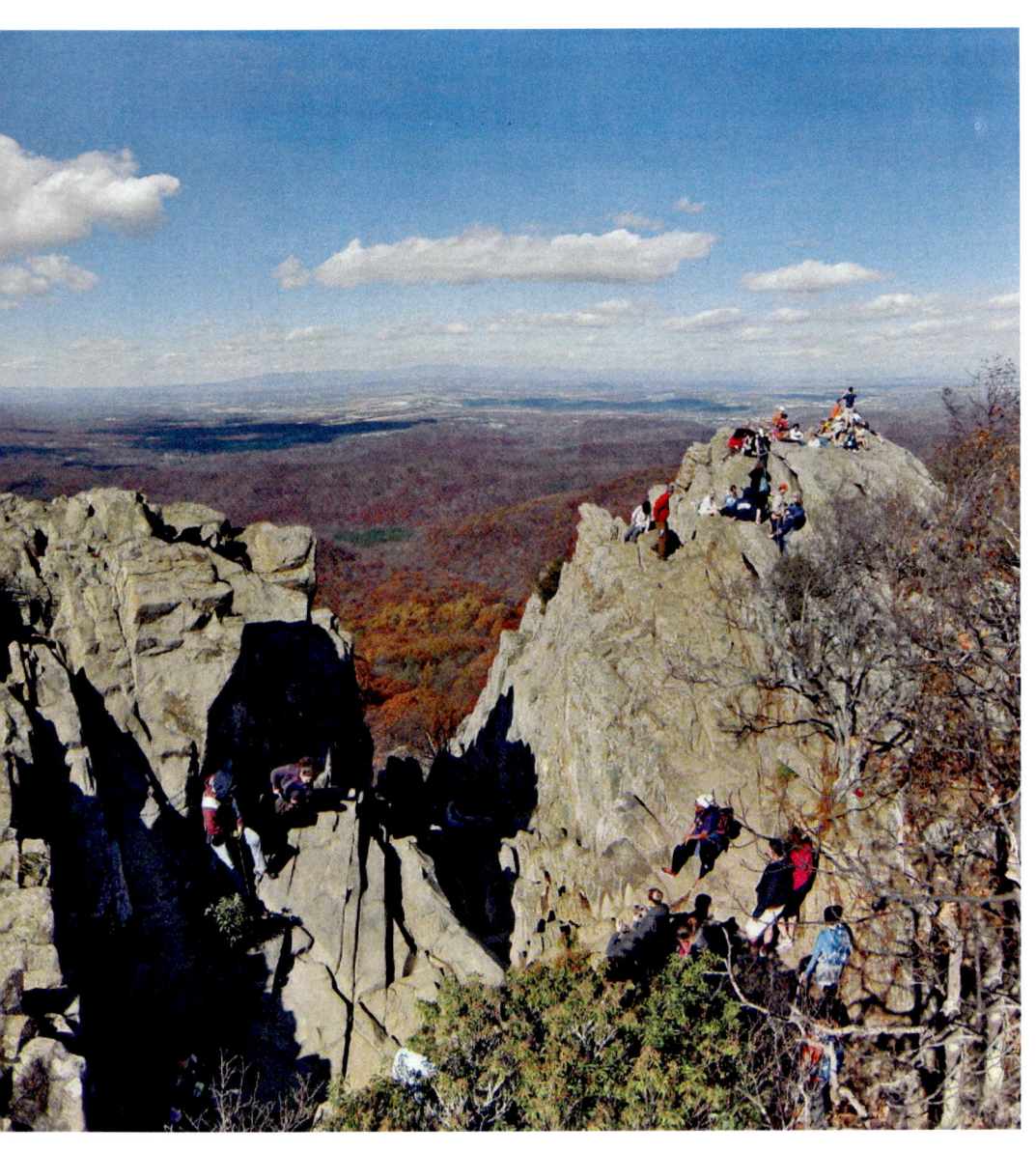

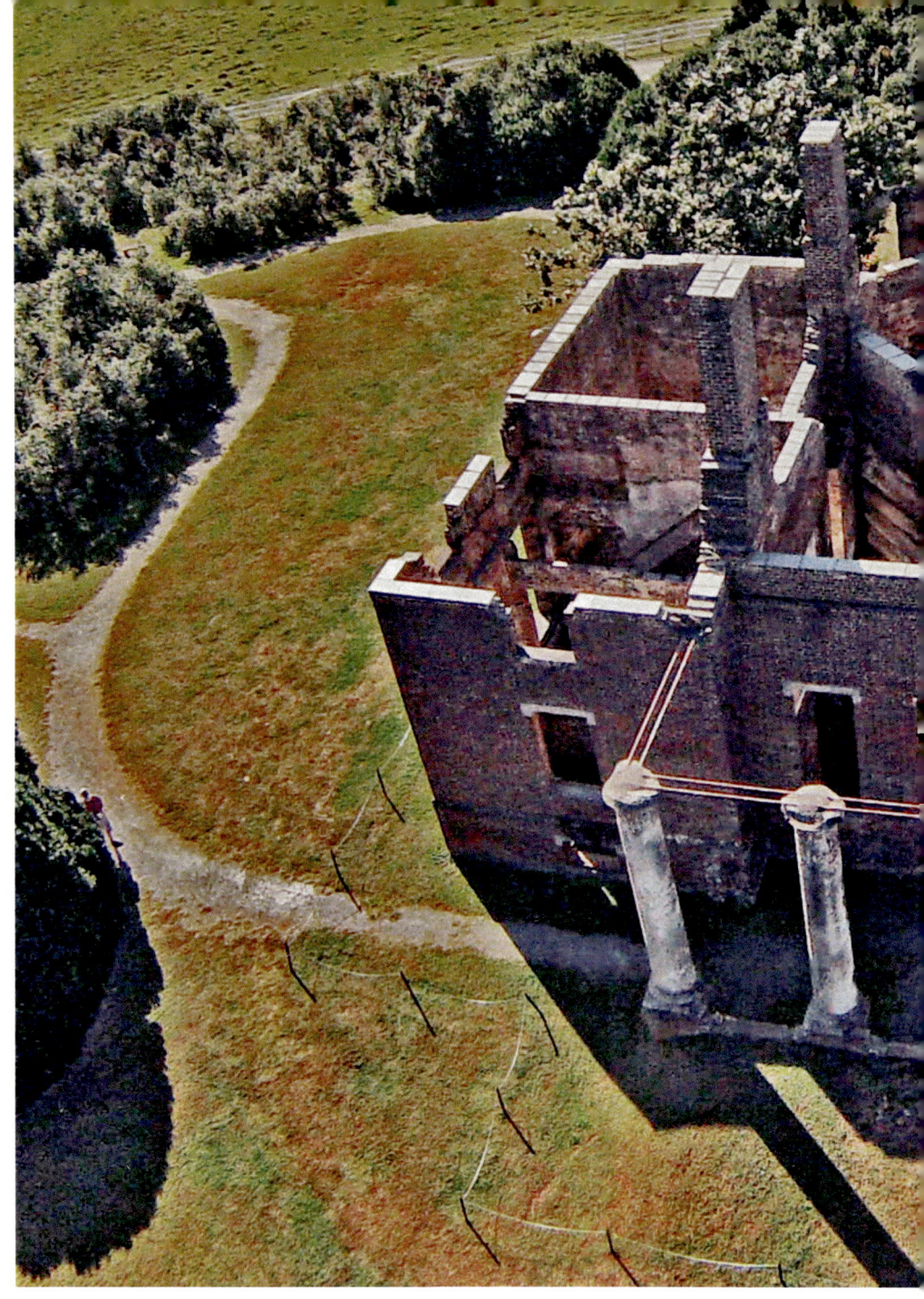

52   Barboursville Ruins (Barboursville Va.)

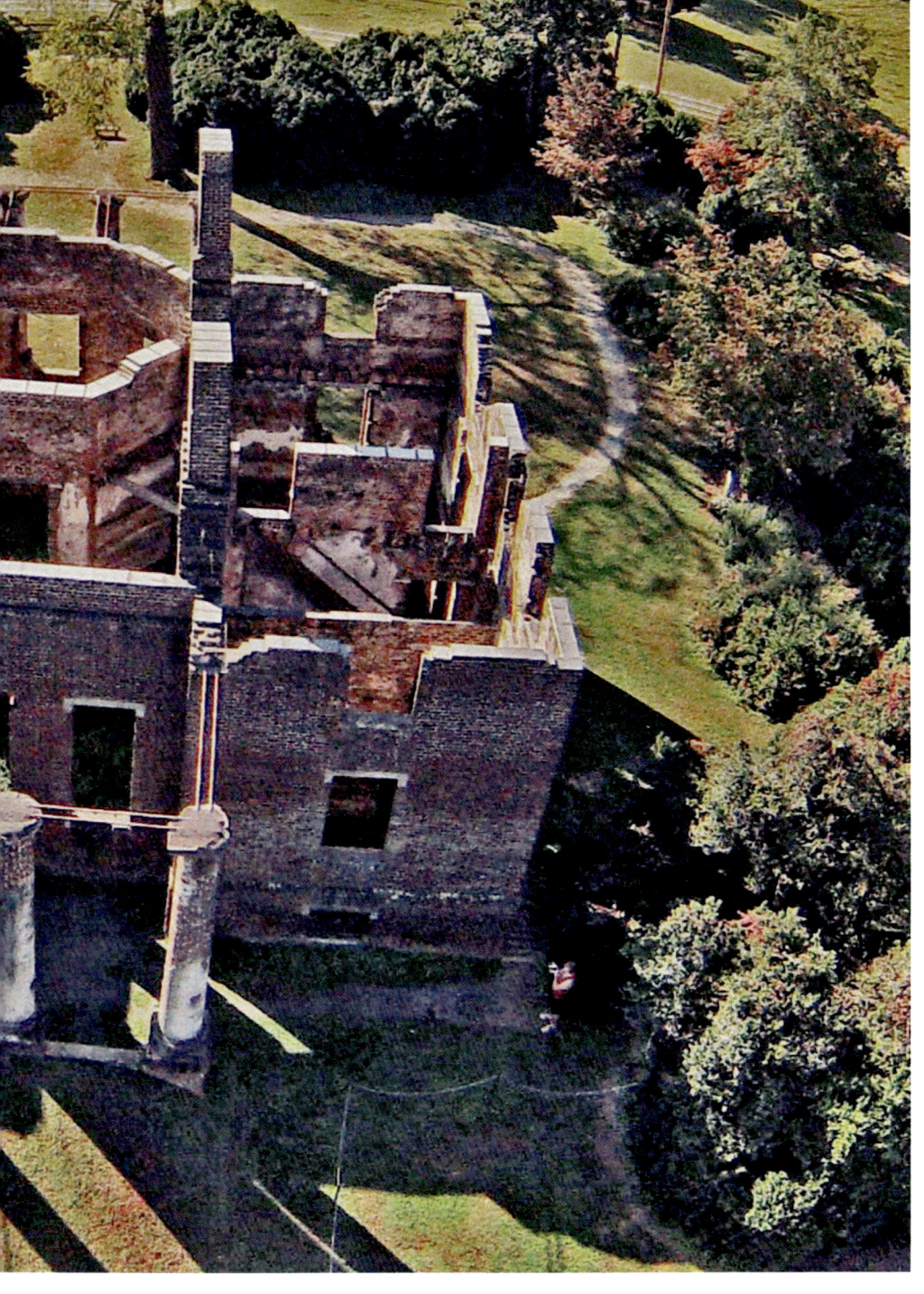

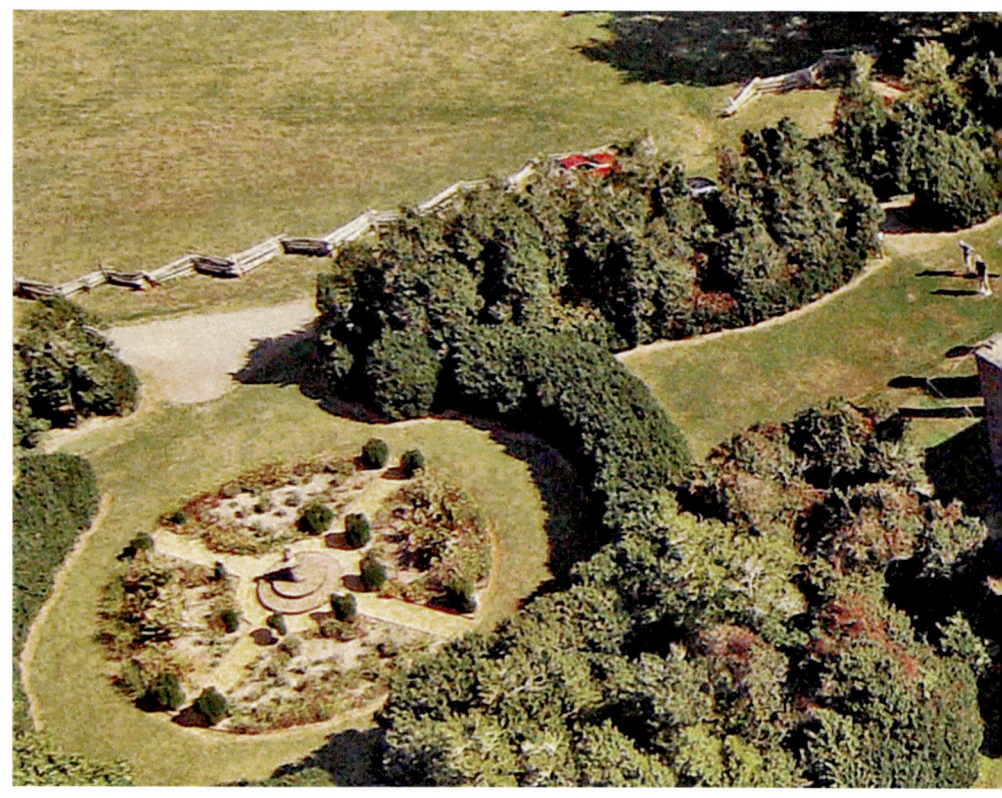

54   Barboursville Ruins (Barboursville Va.)

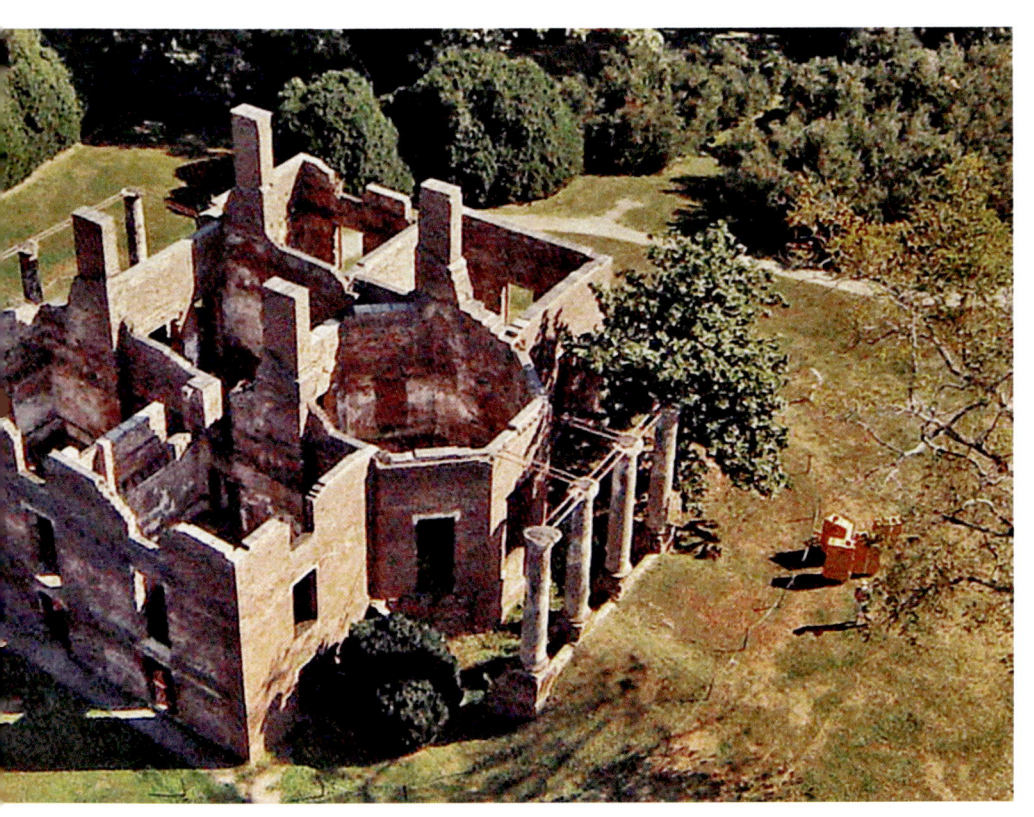

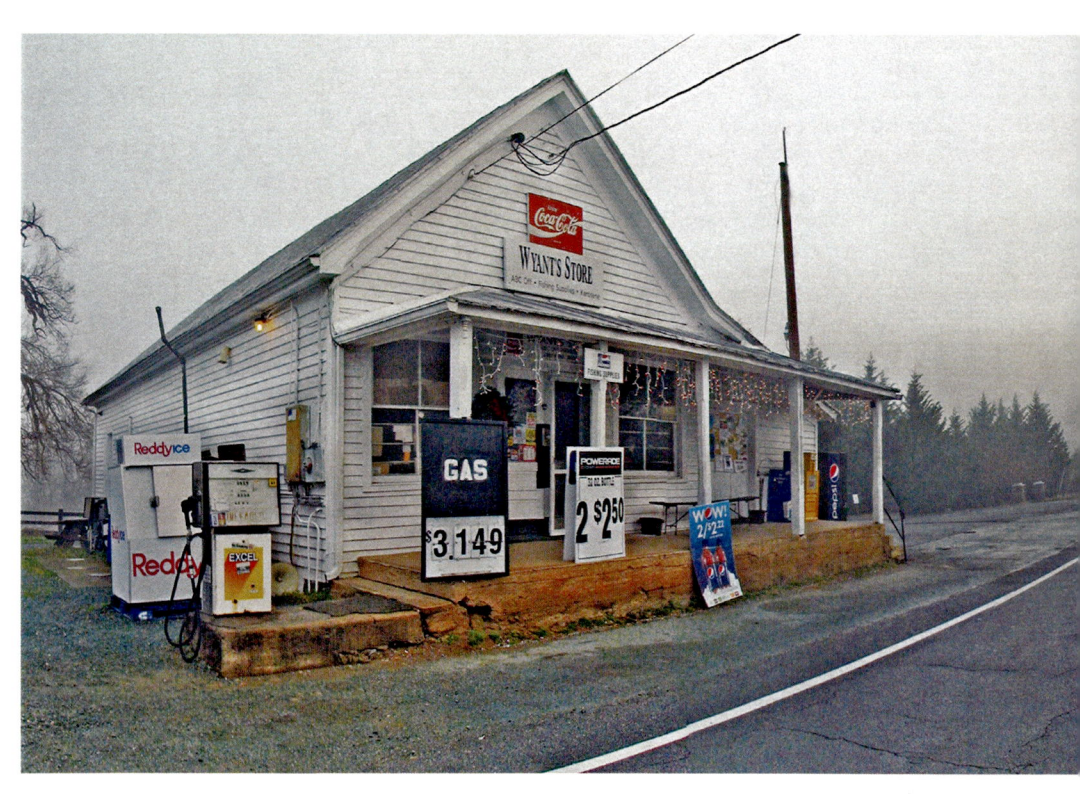

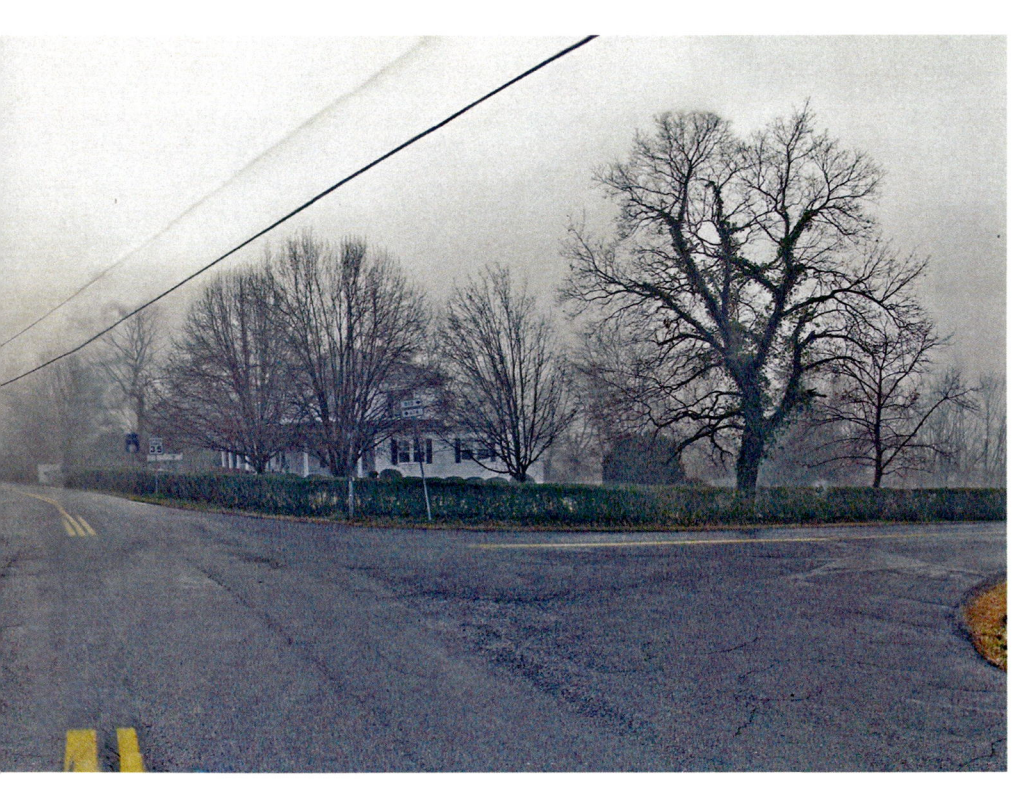

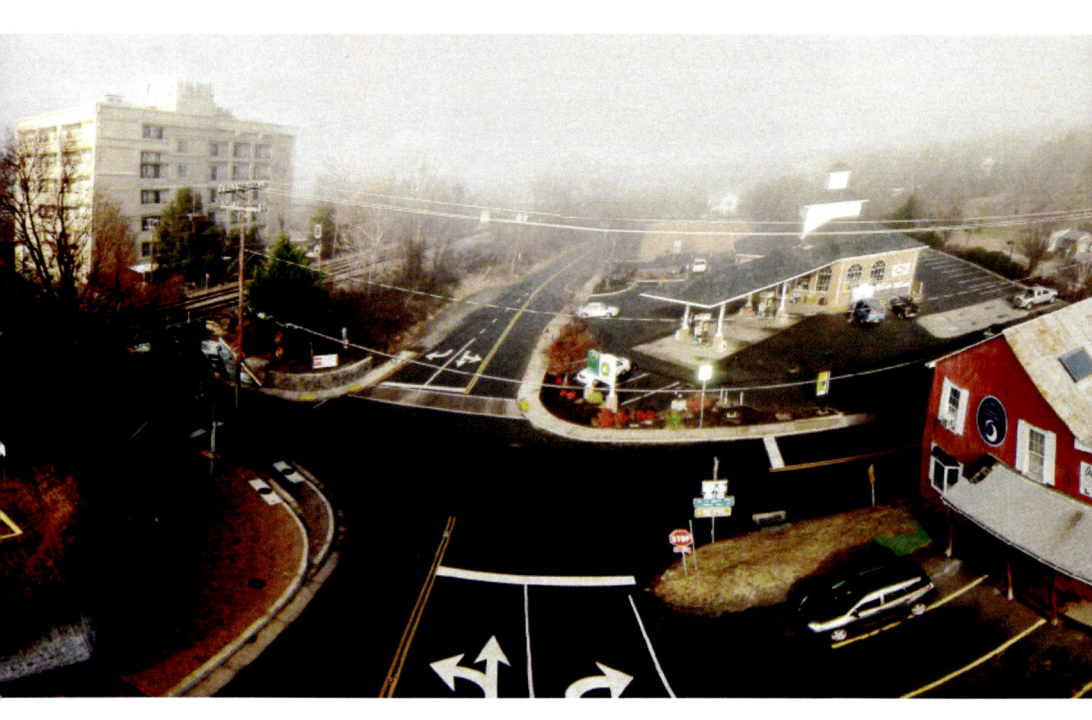

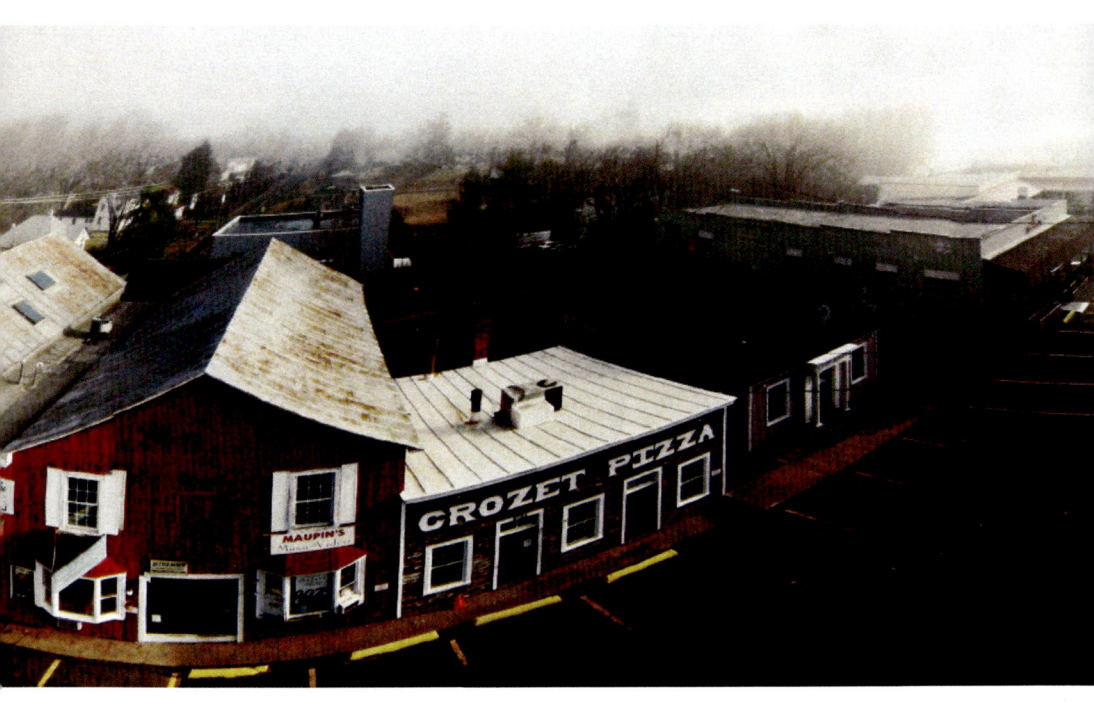

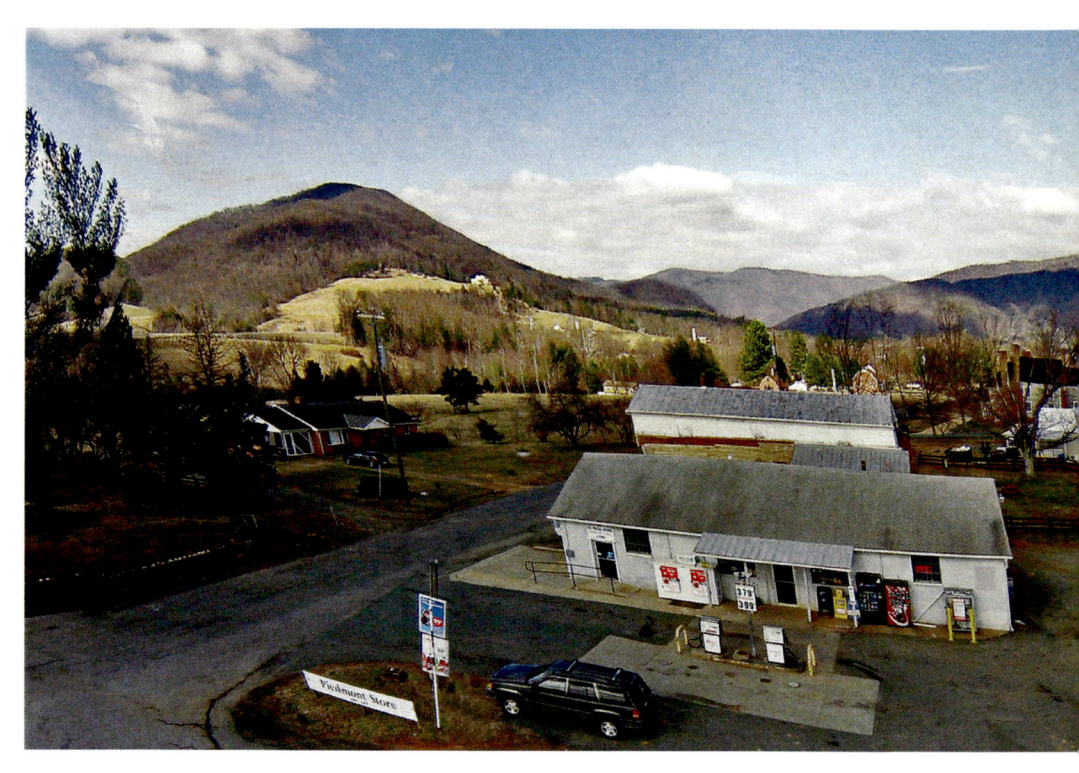

60   Looking West from White Hall Va. towards Sugar Hollow

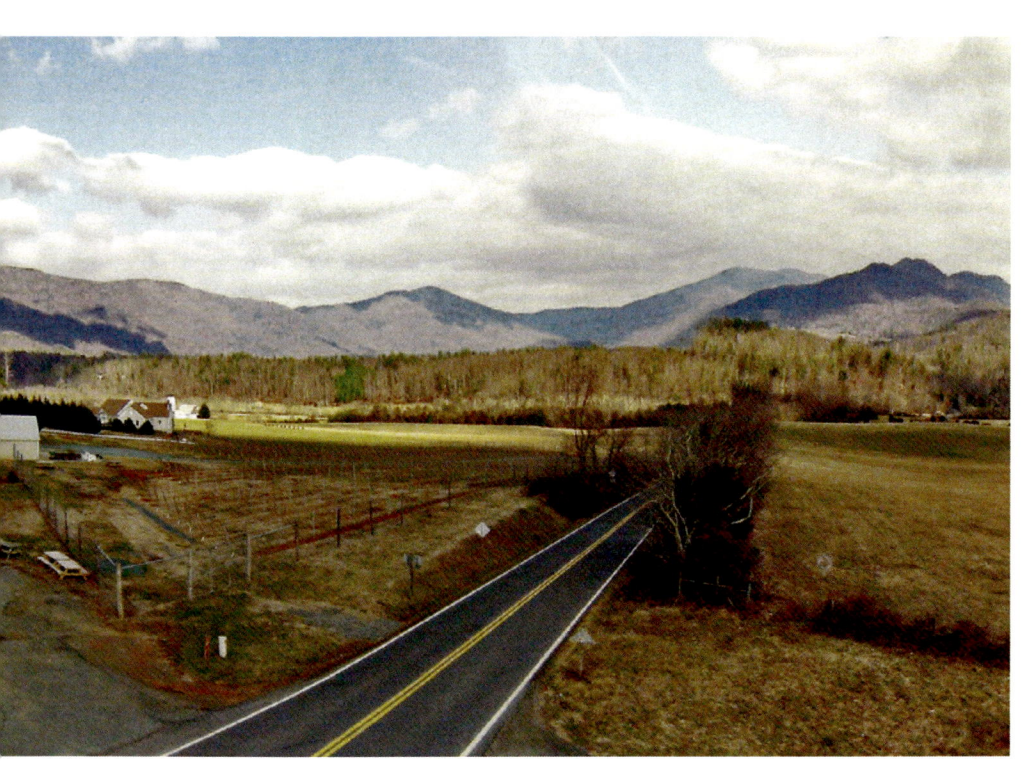

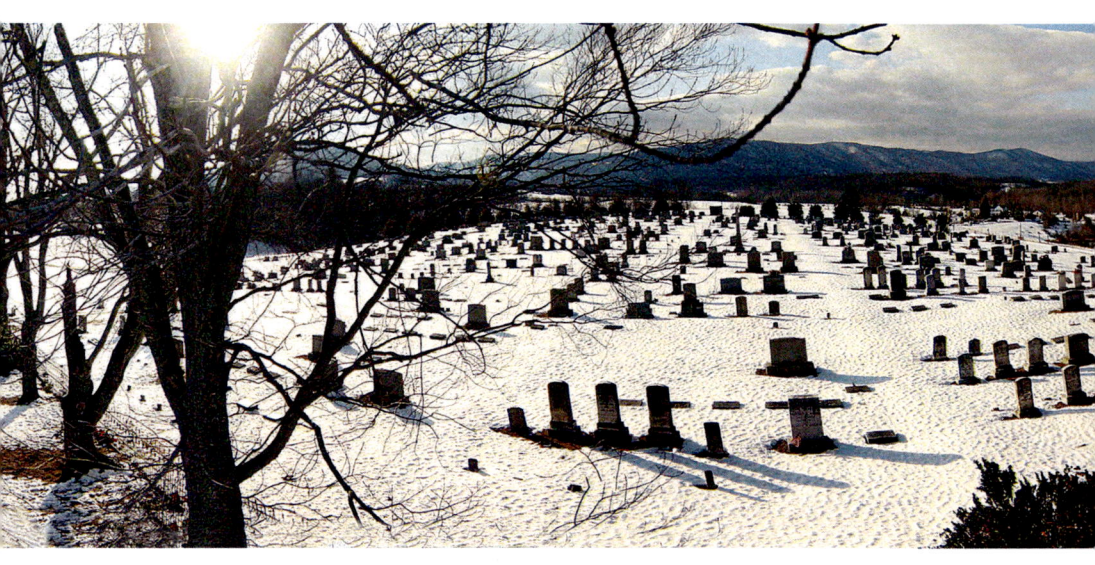

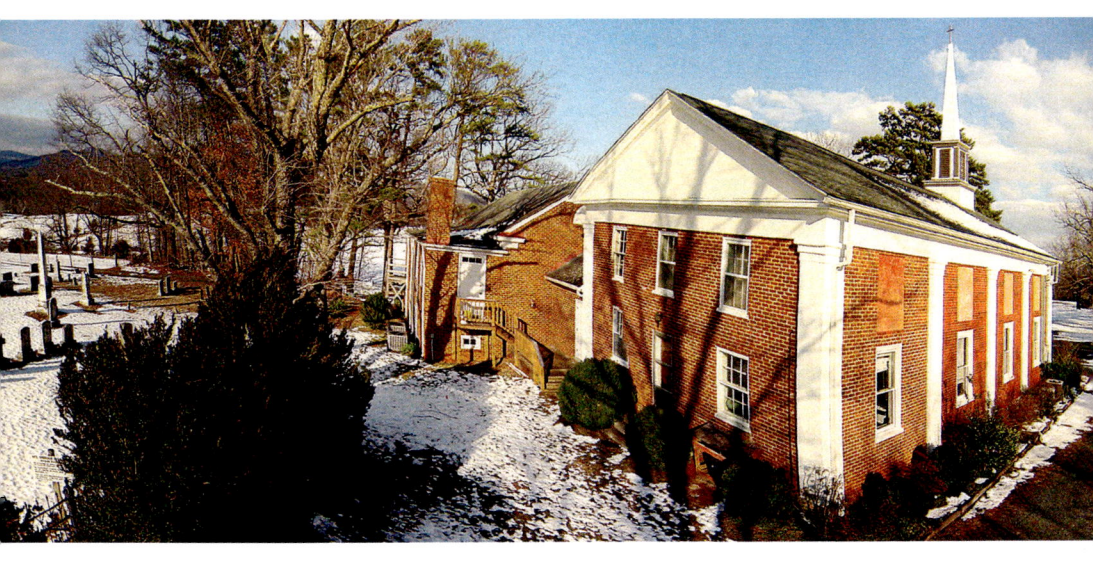

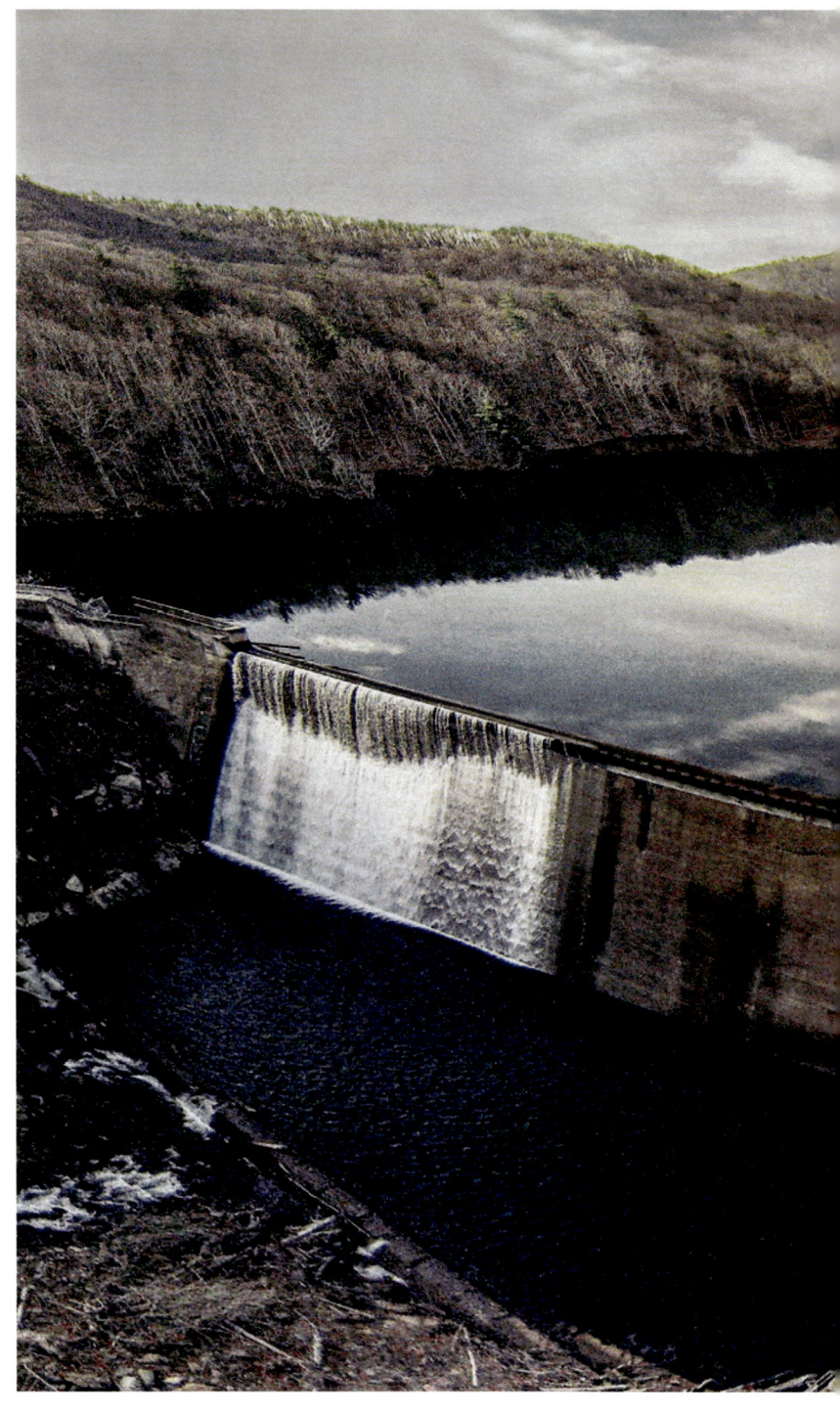

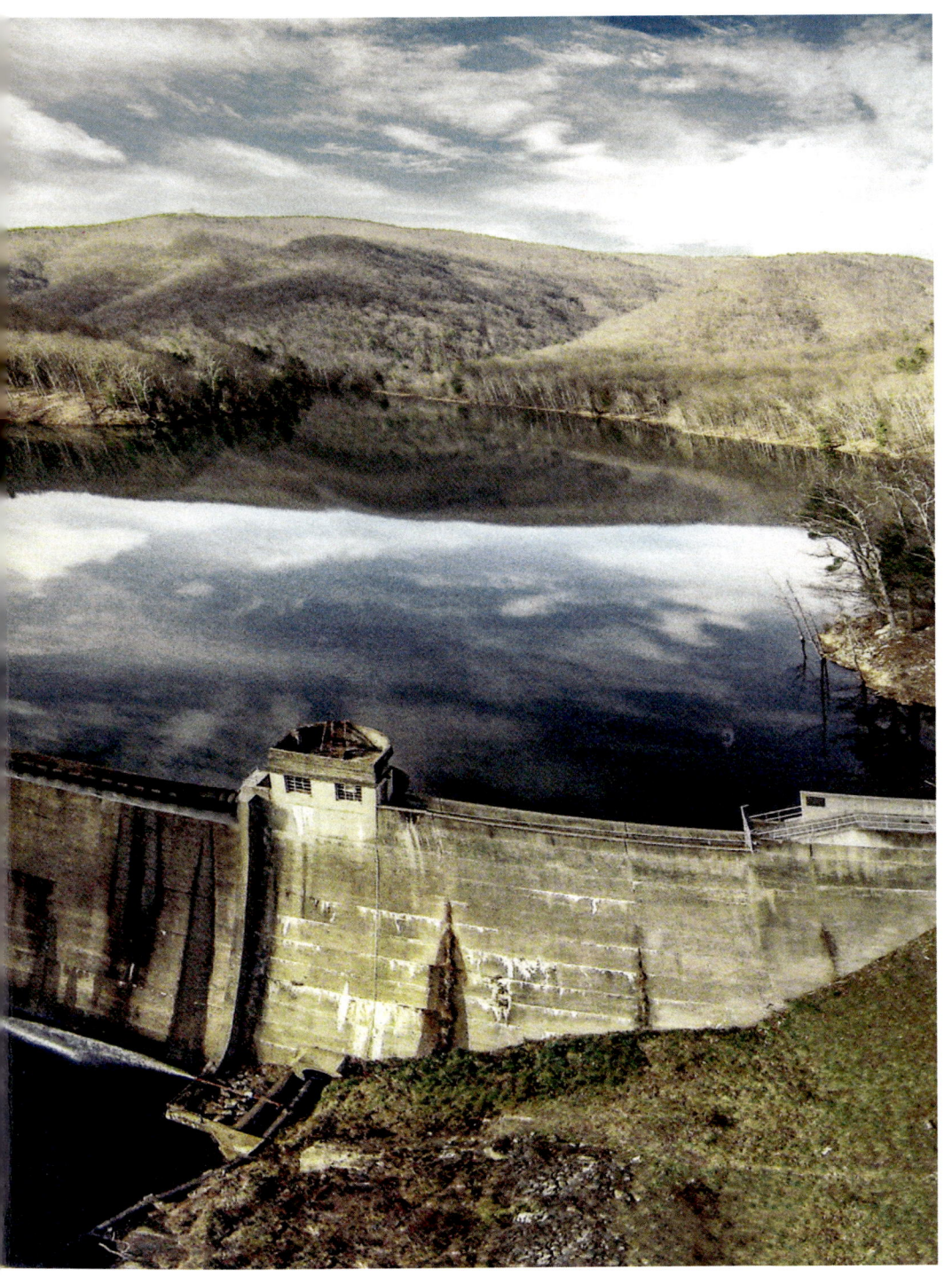

artist John Vigour approaches drone photography as a life-long pilot of remotely-controlled model airplanes. He discovered that the extraordinary stability of multi-rotor aircraft enables one to shoot multiple aligned photographs. What followed was an extended evolution of technique and artistic approach that culminates in this book.